Electrifying a Century

Celebrating 1906-2006 100 Years of Minnesota Power

FIRST EDITION
Published by Minnesota Power, Duluth, Minnesota
Copyright © 2006 by Minnesota Power

Design and Production by
WestmorelandFlint, LLC
Advertising/Marketing/Public Relations

Writer: Bill Beck, Lakeside Writers' Group, Inc.
Photo Editor: Marilyn Weber, Minnesota Power
Archivist: Keith Larson and the Minnesota Power/ALLETE
ITS-Record Services team

Photos in the book are from a collection of visuals used in various publications throughout the years.
Photographers include Sam Alvar, John Coletti, Jeff Frey, Sam Johnston,
Alvis Upitis, Eric Vardakis and Craig Wells.

Library of Congress Control Number
2006925150

International Standard Book Number
0-9747195-4-4

Printed in the United States of America
By Service Printers, Duluth, Minnesota

Table of Contents

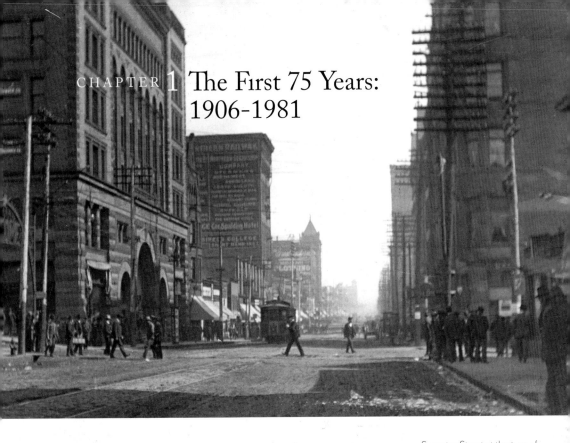

CHAPTER 1 The First 75 Years: 1906-1981

D uluth in 1906 was a thriving, bustling port city striving toward its destiny as the Zenith City of the Unsalted Seas. The community sprawled across some 25 miles of lakeshore, bayfront and riverside development, from Lester River on the northeast to Fond du Lac on the west.

Duluth's population had surpassed 50,000 in the 1900 census, and those in the know assured newcomers that it was already approaching 60,000 people. Jobs were plentiful in what boosters called the "Pittsburgh of the North." Giant U.S. Steel was hiring crews to clear land on the western fringes of the city for a huge new steel mill and company town named after J.P. Morgan, the steel trust's financial wizard. In a day when work was accomplished with manual labor rather than machine, those seeking work need only make the rounds of the city's ore docks, lumber mills, factories and grain

Whaleback steamers and consort barges anchored off Duluth early in the 20th century. When the U.S. Army Corps of Engineers completed its massive harbor improvements in 1908, Duluth-Superior became one of the nation's busiest ports.

elevators. The U.S. Army Corps of Engineers was halfway through a 10-year harbor improvement project that employed hundreds of local residents to man dredges in the harbor and to build the massive concrete and stone breakwaters jutting into Lake Superior off Canal Park.

Daily life in the city was a cacophony of sounds. Foghorns tooted, ship whistles screamed, bells clanged, sawmills buzzed and steam whistles shrieked. In an era when smoke abatement was yet to be considered a laudable goal, Duluth and neighboring Superior often were shrouded in thick haze, the product of a society that burned coal and wood for heat, cooking and to power steam engines.

The Duluth Edison

In 1906, technological change was coming to the Twin Ports in the form of more widespread use of electric power. The magic of commercially available electricity was only about 25 years removed from Thomas Edison's experiment with generation and transmission at the Pearl Street Station in Lower Manhattan. In that quarter-century, arc lighting and incandescent electric systems had made their way into just about every city and town in North America.

Thomas Edison in his Menlo Park, New Jersey laboratory about 1900.

Most systems were sold as franchises of the Edison General Electric patents or by representatives of the nation's other electric manufacturers of the early 20th century, usually the Thomson-Houston Company or the Westinghouse Company. The entrepreneurs responsible for electrifying Duluth in the 1890s and early 1900s were brothers Otto and Alexander Hartman and their brother-in-law, Curtis Van Bergen.

The Hartman brothers had homesteaded a log cabin above the Point of Rocks in the late 1870s and had amassed fortunes in Duluth's booming private enterprise. During the 1880s, Alexander Hartman was general agent of the Northern Pacific Railway; his brother, Otto, was president of the Duluth Board of Trade.

In 1888, the Hartmans incorporated the Duluth Electric Company to provide arc lighting to their hometown. They installed generators and boilers in a former grain elevator building at Fourth Avenue East and the lakeshore and started wiring the growing city. In the 1890s, they joined with Minneapolis electric utility entrepreneur H.M. Byllesby to buy out a competitor and form the Hartman Electric Company. In 1893, the Hartmans and Van Bergen built the Commerce Street Station, Duluth's major source of electric power for the next 14 years.

Providing electric power has always been a capital intensive endeavor, and the Hartman brothers struggled with finances for much of the 1890s and early 1900s. The Hartmans had organized a holding company in 1896, Commercial Light and Power Company, to consolidate Duluth's electric, gas and water utilities under one corporate ownership structure. But Commercial Light and Power almost immediately found itself overextended.

Alexander Hartman's Commerce Street Station provided the bulk of Duluth's electric power in the early 1900s.

In 1897, the Duluth City Council issued bonds and agreed to purchase the water and gas properties from Commercial. In the summer of 1898, the City established a Light and Water Board which attempted over the next 20 years to bring the Hartman brothers' electric utility under City control.

A predecessor to Minnesota Power, the Duluth Edison Electric Company might well have ended up as a municipal utility had it not been for a courtly Alabamian, Sydney Zollicoffer Mitchell. Named for a pair of Confederate generals, Mitchell in 1905 convinced Charles Coffin of General Electric to create a GE holding company that would oversee the affairs of the dozens of electric utilities that GE had loaned money to during the preceding 20 years. Because electric utilities were so capital intensive, GE had wound up with stocks and bonds of utilities from all over the United States. Typically, the stocks, bonds and liens had been offered

Duluthians early on established a habit of supporting the local electric company by purchasing its common stock.

in partial payment for General Electric equipment or franchise fees.

General Electric had taken an ownership position in the Hartmans' utility in 1896 at the time of the formation of Commercial Light and Power. In 1900, Commercial had filed bankruptcy and was reorganized as the Duluth General Electric Co., still under the control of the Hartmans and Curtis Van Bergen.

Five years later, the firm again was strapped for cash to keep up with the growth of Duluth. Sydney Z. Mitchell stepped in and made Duluth General Electric one of the first operating utilities of his new holding company, the Electric Bond and Share Company. The utility was reorganized in the late winter of 1906 as the Duluth Edison Electric Company, the direct predecessor of what would become Minnesota Power and ALLETE.

The Great Northern Power Connection

The 1906 formation of Duluth Edison Electric coincided with the completion of one of the more ambitious hydroelectric projects on the North American continent. Great Northern Power Company's

An army of workers swarmed onto the Thomson Dam construction site in 1906 to build one of the biggest hydroelectric projects in America at the time for the Great Northern Power Company.

construction of the Thomson high dam at the Dalles of the St. Louis River west of Duluth was nearing its close in 1906. When finished and placed into commercial operation in 1907, Thomson would make available to Duluth Edison Electric what seemed at the time to be limitless, inexpensive electric power.

Thomson was the culmination of dreams to harness the abundant hydroelectric resources of the St. Louis River that went back more than 30 years. As early as the 1870s, Jay Cooke, the Philadelphia financier who had underwritten President Abraham Lincoln's armies during the Civil War, had envisioned a series of power dams and reservoirs on the St. Louis that would have turned Duluth into one of the manufacturing capitals of the continent. Cooke's dreams had been dashed by the Panic of 1873, but others had taken up the vision of a vast hydroelectric system designed to feed the demand for electric power in Duluth and the mines of the nearby Iron Ranges.

The 1892 opening of the Mesabi Range, with enormous reserves of rich, red iron ore, spurred a number of schemes for tapping the hydroelectric potential of the watershed north and west of Duluth. In 1893, the Minnesota Canal and Power Company proposed building a dam across the Kawishiwi River, creating a storage reservoir at Birch Lake and diverting water into the Embarrass River, a tributary of the St. Louis. Minnesota Canal and Power put forward plans to build a second dam on the St. Louis above Cloquet, backing up the river's water into a reservoir that would reach all the way to the Duluth Heights neighborhood. Water then would be piped down hill to hydroelectric generators at 15th Avenue West in the Zenith City.

At the turn of the 20th century, the Highland Canal and Power Company suggested a variation of the earlier plans, creating a series of storage reservoirs along the St. Louis and piping the water from the last reservoir down hill into Duluth. The president of Highland Canal and Power was Alexander McDougall, a Scottish immigrant who had made his mark building whaleback steamers at a ship yard across the Bay in Superior.

The Thomson Dam backed up the St. Louis River into a forebay, which sent water downhill through a redwood pipe, called a penstock, to the generators at the hydroelectric station far below.

One of the major investors in Highland Canal and Power was Charles C. Cokefair, a Wall Street venture capitalist, and his son, Frank, a Columbia University-trained hydraulic engineer. The Cokefairs eventually incorporated the Great Northern Power Company as a successor to several of the earlier hydroelectric designs. They offered a scaled-down version of the plans advanced by Minnesota Canal and Power and Highland Canal and Power. Great Northern Power recommended building a dam across the St. Louis at Thomson west of Duluth, a hydroelectric station nearby and a high-voltage transmission line to a brick substation at 15th Avenue West in Duluth.

In 1905, Great Northern Power Company signed a contract with the Hartmans to provide wholesale electric power to the then Duluth General Electric Company. Construction on the $4 million Thomson Hydro project got underway that spring. By that time, the Cokefairs were simply managers for the New York banks that were financing the project. When Thomson began delivering commercial power in the fall of 1907, young Frank Cokefair already had left the Twin Ports for another hydroelectric project in the Pacific Northwest.

The first 50 years of the history of St. Louis County was dominated by economic circumstances beyond the control of the local community. The Panic of 1857 all but depopulated the tiny villages that would later combine to create the city of Duluth. The Panic of 1873 derailed Jay Cooke's plans to develop the resources of northeastern Minnesota. The Panic of 1893 ensured that future development of the region's immense iron ore deposits would be controlled by business interests headquartered in Pittsburgh, Cleveland and New York, rather than Duluth.

Financial disaster almost struck the region again in 1907. The Knickerbocker Trust Company, one of the underwriters of the Thomson Hydro project, failed just one month after Thomson went on line and precipitated the Panic of 1907. Fortunately, power already was flowing to the substation at 15th Avenue West.

Consolidation

Duluth Edison Electric and Great Northern Power Company, two of the most important direct antecedents of Minnesota Power, grew separately between 1907 and 1922. Great Northern Power generated electric power for wholesale purchase by other utilities or industries. Duluth Edison Electric, on the other hand, distributed power it purchased from other entities to its residential customers.

Since its consolidation by the Electric Bond and Share Company in 1923, Minnesota Power has occupied its headquarters at 30 West Superior Street in Duluth.

Duluth Edison Electric had turned into a profitable venture for Electric Bond and Share Company, so profitable that the City of Duluth renewed its campaign to municipalize the Duluth utility. Led by Leonidas "Lon" Merritt, the Duluth City Commission waged a two-year fight to acquire control of the utility from the Hartmans and Electric Bond and Share.

Duluth's growth had continued unabated during the early years of the 20th century. The city's population was nearly 80,000 by 1910, and grew to just under 100,000 by 1920. The city's voters went to the polls in 1915 to decide whether the city or the Hartmans would control Duluth's electric utility. Duluth Edison Electric won the special election by a margin of 270 votes out of more than 9,000 cast.

With the onset of World War I, Duluth Edison Electric continued to expand to serve the city's growing population and its collection of critical war industries. The utility was tested as never before in the fall of 1918 when many in its work force were stricken by the influenza pandemic that killed hundreds in northeastern Minnesota. Even worse, much of the utility's distribution system in Lester Park and Lakeside was destroyed by the Moose Lake forest fire in October 1918.

The then Minnesota Power & Light Company began providing its line workers with specialized trucks as early as the 1920s.

Still, Duluth Edison Electric emerged from the war years as a thriving, prosperous utility. In 1922, the company posted revenues of more than $1 million and had 22,500 customers. Late that year, Electric Bond and Share decided to make Duluth Edison Electric the cornerstone of a consolidated utility which would serve residential, industrial and commercial customers across a broad swath of northern Minnesota.

The holding company's business strategy in the 1920s called for the creation of integrated utilities that combined generation, transmission and distribution systems in one regional system. Sydney Z. Mitchell strongly believed in the benefits of diversity, reasoning that a utility serving as broad a constituency of customer classes as possible would be insulated from economic downturns affecting one of those customer groups.

The Little Falls and Blanchard hydroelectric facilities on the Mississippi River extended Minnesota Power's electric service in the 1920s well into west central Minnesota.

The integration of utilities was helped in the 1920s by advances in transmission line technologies. What the engineers called the "high line" had increased dramatically in voltage and carrying power during World War I and after. The introduction of 69,000-volt, 110,000-volt and 138,000-volt transmission lines allowed small-town utilities to interconnect to base load generating stations and significantly decreased the kilowatt-hour cost of electricity during the

1920s. Lower cost electricity created more demand, which in turn allowed integrated utilities to build bigger, more efficient generating stations.

In October 1923, Electric Bond and Share announced the incorporation of Minnesota Power & Light Company. Immediately known to generations of northeastern Minnesota residents as MP&L, the new utility was a combination of Duluth Edison Electric and Great Northern Power Company, both of which Electric Bond and Share controlled. The holding company also purchased several other smaller northern Minnesota utilities, including the Minnesota Utilities Company on the Mesabi Range, the General Light and Power Company in Cloquet, the Little Falls Water Power Company and the Cuyuna Range Power Company.

In the 1930s, Minnesota Power made a special effort to acquaint customers with the labor-saving benefits of electric appliances.

In 1924, the new utility had revenues of $4.5 million and operated four different divisions: Central, Cloquet, Little Falls and the Range. In announcing MP&L's formation, Electric Bond and Share noted that the new utility immediately would embark on a $15 million construction program. From 1923 to 1928, MP&L built the Fond du Lac Hydroelectric station on the St. Louis River, Blanchard Hydroelectric Station on the Mississippi River and the Winton Hydroelectric Station on the Kawishiwi River. Utility crews also constructed a 110,000-volt transmission grid to interconnect the new hydro plants.

MP&L quickly established a reputation for its sales ability. MP&L engineers worked closely with iron mining customers on the Mesabi Range to electrify many of the Range's mining functions during the 1920s. The utility also established a flourishing business selling and maintaining electric appliances for the home during the decade.

Depression and War

For MP&L and its nearly 1,000 employees, the stock market crash of the last week of October 1929 ushered in a tumultuous 20 years of depression, war and recovery.

The Great Depression of the 1930s was a period of monetary deflation and was exacerbated by unemployment in many industries, mostly in the manufacturing sector. Utilities in general, and MP&L in particular, weren't as impacted by conditions as other businesses. It is an irony of the electric power business that MP&L revenues actually grew during the Great Depression. The reason was twofold. Those northeastern Minnesota residents who did have jobs, for example, bought electric appliances for the home and office. And those electric appliances, which increased the demand curve for MP&L, cost less to purchase as the decade of the 1930s wore on, thanks mostly to the price deflation that was so prevalent at the time. In addition, mining iron ore wasn't as energy intensive a process as it later became. As a result, MP&L wasn't as vulnerable to economic conditions in the iron mining industry as it would later become.

MP&L did its part to help alleviate the unemployment that was ravaging Duluth and northeastern Minnesota. In 1930, Electric Bond and Share authorized a massive construction program at its operating utilities nationwide. A secondary purpose of the program was to put the unemployed to work, and MP&L immediately hired hundreds of workers to begin the construction of a $3 million, coal-fired steam electric generating station on the bayfront in West Duluth. In less than one year, the first unit of the 25,000-kilowatt generating station was providing electric power to the MP&L system.

The election of President Franklin D. Roosevelt in 1932 brought unprecedented change to the electric utility industry. Roosevelt's New Deal administration passed legislation that brought electric power to the nation's farms and created the Tennessee Valley Authority to produce electricity and economic development in one of the nation's most impoverished regions.

Once Minnesota Utilities Company was consolidated into Minnesota Power in 1923, electrification of Minnesota's iron mining industry accelerated. By the 1930s, literally all of the Mesabi mines were powered by electricity.

In 1935, Roosevelt successfully broke up the holding companies. MP&L, along with dozens of other operating utilities, was restructured and ordered spun off in an initial public offering on the New York Stock Exchange.

Before that IPO could take place, MP&L and its people helped America defeat the Axis in World War II. The Japanese attack on the American Naval base at Pearl Harbor, Hawaii, on December 7, 1941, caught much of society off guard. But MP&L had already begun to ramp up its production of electric power in 1940, the year that Roosevelt began transferring obsolete destroyers to Great Britain under the Lend Lease Program. The Company's kilowatt-hour sales increased one-third between

1940 and 1941, as the Mesabi Iron Range increased its production of iron ore for the nation's defense needs.

Under the leadership of M.L. Hibbard, MP&L in 1942 was able to double the size of the West Duluth Steam Electric Station when the War Department designated the plant a critical war asset. Still primarily a hydroelectric utility, MP&L nevertheless provided the electric power that allowed the nearly 50 iron mines on the Mesabi, Cuyuna and Vermilion Ranges to operate at peak production during the war. Between 1941 and 1945, Minnesota's iron mines shipped almost a half-billion tons of red ore down the Lakes for America's war effort. The utility and its subsidiary, Superior Water Light & Power, also provided the electric power to a booming shipbuilding industry in the Twin Ports.

During the 1940s, the Minnesota Power home service advisor became a valued member of the communities of northeastern Minnesota.

MP&L kept the electric grid of northeastern Minnesota operating flawlessly during the war, in spite of the struggle to find material and manpower to keep the system maintained. By 1945, some 20 percent of MP&L's pre-war work force were in uniform, serving on the far-flung war fronts across the world. Back home, MP&L employees bought war bonds, planted Victory Gardens, coped with ration cards and sewed bandages in Red Cross classes.

The Japanese surrender in the summer of 1945 was greeted with a collective sigh of relief. But for MP&L, it was business as usual. The pent up demand for homes, cars and appliances from returning veterans anxious to start families kicked off an economic boom unprecedented in the nation's history.

Postwar Boom

MP&L underwent a significant transformation during the late 1940s. With the addition of a new 35,000-kilowatt generator at West Duluth's renamed M.L. Hibbard Steam Electric Station, the utility made a pronounced shift from hydroelectric to steam generation. Industrial sales continued very strong in the late 1940s and early 1950s, as the United

States remained on a war footing through the early years of the Cold War and the outbreak of the Korean Conflict in 1951. But residential usage doubled and doubled again between 1945 and 1959. Residential customers were using just over 4,000 kilowatts a year in 1959, and paying 2.74 cents per kilowatt-hour.

MP&L unveiled an aggressive building project to meet the growing demand for electric power. In 1950, crews began clearing a site on Colby Lake just east of Aurora for a new power plant that would nearly double the utility's capacity. When the Aurora Steam Generating Station was brought on line in 1953, it boasted generating capacity of 88,000 kilowatts. The plant on the eastern end of the Mesabi Range later would be named in honor of Sylvester Laskin, MP&L's CEO during the 1960s and 1970s.

Construction of the Aurora Steam Electric Station in the early 1950s was a concrete symbol of Minnesota Power's faith in the future growth of the eastern Mesabi Range.

Less than two years after the Aurora Station began the commercial generation of power, MP&L began seeking another site for a new steam generation plant. The utility's engineers sought a location on the western end of the Mesabi Range that would interconnect the MP&L system in a triangle. The Hibbard Station in West Duluth would anchor the south end of the system, the Aurora Station would anchor the east end of the system, and the new station would anchor the west end of MP&L's system.

The site selected for the new power plant was at Cohasset in Itasca County, just west of Grand Rapids. Clay C. Boswell, MP&L's president & CEO, whose name would grace the new plant, joined Cohasset Mayor Harvey Avenson in the plant's groundbreaking on April 24, 1956. Initially planned for one unit with generation capacity of 65,000 kilowatts, Clay Boswell Station was almost immediately doubled in size. By the time the first two units were dedicated in 1960, northeastern Minnesota was undergoing a technological revolution.

Construction crews moved onto the site near Cohasset of what would become the Boswell Steam Electric Station, Minnesota Power's largest generating facility, in the summer of 1956.

Taconite

When World War II ended in 1945, officials of America's iron mining industry worried that dwindling reserves of natural ore from the Lake Superior region would be supplanted by immense new deposits of iron ore developed during the war in Canada, South America and West Africa. The tremendous consumption of iron ore from the Minnesota Ranges during World War II and the Korean Conflict did deplete Minnesota's vast stocks of natural ore. But reports of the demise of Minnesota's iron mining economy were wildly exaggerated.

Minnesota Power and its employees—shown here at a company rally—urged Minnesota's residents to support the 1964 Taconite Amendment with a resounding "yes" vote.

E.W. Davis, a professor at the University of Minnesota Mines Experiment Station in the Twin Cities, had been researching the commercial development of taconite since 1912. Taconite is a low grade iron ore that underlay much of the Mesabi Iron Range. Estimates suggested billions of tons of the hard, flinty iron rock could be dug from Minnesota pits.

Davis devised a method of crushing the taconite rock, separating the iron powder from the tailings with electro-magnets and binding the resulting concentrate with clay. Davis then rolled the concentrate into marble-sized pellets and fired them in a kiln at 2,500 degrees Fahrenheit. The resulting pellets were 66 percent iron and created a charge in steel mill blast furnaces that was more even and easier for metallurgists to control. By the mid-1950s, Erie Mining Company near Hoyt Lakes and Reserve Mining Company at Silver Bay were the first two commercial taconite facilities on Minnesota's Mesabi Range.

Taconite processing used immense amounts of electric power to grind, separate and concentrate the pellets. Early taconite facilities used as much as 100 kilowatt-hours of electricity to produce one ton of pellets, some 20 times the amount of electric power used to produce a ton of natural ore.

The first taconite companies elected to build generating plants dedicated to the production of pellets. As other steel companies saw how efficient pellets were in the blast furnaces, they began to investigate the construction of processing mills in Minnesota themselves. In 1963, MP&L established a new industrial rate that was less than a cent per kilowatt-hour. When Minnesota voters passed the Taconite Amendment in 1964, establishing an equitable mining tax rate, the steel industry embarked on a taconite building boom in northeastern Minnesota.

In 1965, MP&L agreed to serve Eveleth Taconite, National Steel Pellet Company, Butler Taconite and U.S. Steel's planned Minntac Plant. After studying the most efficient use of the utility's generating resources, MP&L engineers announced plans to build a third unit at Boswell Station. At 350 megawatts, the new unit was more than twice the size of the plant's two existing units.

The taconite boom turned MP&L into a construction company. Contracted taconite load totaled 231,000 kilowatts in 1972. But then the taconite industry underwent another growth spurt. U.S. Steel, National Steel Pellet and Eveleth Taconite all announced major expansions during the 1970s. Hibbing Taconite and Inland Steel's Minorca plant added another 8 million tons of pellet capacity. By 1979, MP&L's taconite power supply demand had more than tripled from early in the decade, to 683,000 kilowatts.

The rapid increase in industrial load led to several major construction projects during the decade. MP&L added a fourth unit at Boswell, a 500,000-kilowatt generator that was nearly double the size of any other unit on the utility's system. MP&L also became a joint venture partner in Square Butte Electric Cooperative, a mine-mouth generating station in the lignite fields of North Dakota. MP&L brought power back east from Square Butte via an innovative, high-voltage direct current transmission line.

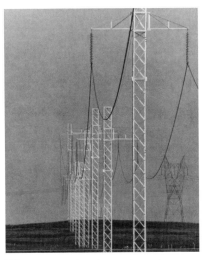

When taconite plants began demanding ever-larger amounts of electric power capacity, Minnesota Power built an innovative "coal by wire" direct current high-voltage transmission line from the lignite fields of North Dakota to northeastern Minnesota.

By 1979, MP&L was planning a massive, new coal-fired generating station at Floodwood-Fine Lakes, just west of the Twin Ports. Revenues and kilowatt-hour production had been on an ever upward trend for more than 20 years, and taconite production was at record levels.

And then the bottom fell out of America's iron and steel industry.

CHAPTER 2 The Wolf at the Door

The late summer of 1979 was one of the prettiest old-timers could remember. Summer had started slowly, with ice still in the Duluth harbor after the first of June, but from July to mid-September, the gentle breezes from the southwest took hold across the region. The walleyes were hitting from Island Lake north to the Boundary Waters Canoe Area. The string of warm, sunny days and abundant late afternoon and evening rainfall produced a bumper crop of tomatoes in gardens from Little Falls to Aurora-Hoyt Lakes.

Minnesota Power was closing in on the completion of its massive Clay Boswell Unit 4 coal-fired power plant near Cohasset, west of Grand Rapids. The 500-megawatt unit was the largest the Company had ever built, and would enter commercial operation in 1980. Minnesota Power was delighted that the new unit was going to be completed under its construction budget of $400 million, which meant that the Company likely would not have to go to its ratepayers for additional rate relief during the 1980s.

The completion of Unit 4 at Clay Boswell Station near Cohasset in 1980 wrapped up more than 30 years of Minnesota Power's postwar construction program.

In the northern part of Minnesota Power's service territory, construction crews were busy in 1979 finishing the last portions of a 500,000-volt transmission project

that would interconnect Minnesota Power, Northern States Power and Manitoba Hydro. The 500-mile line ran from a substation near Winnipeg southeast to the U.S. border, where it crossed into Minnesota just west of Lake of the Woods and then angled southeast to a Minnesota Power substation on the Mesabi Iron Range. From there, the line dropped south to an NSP substation in the Twin Cities. The Canadian intertie made hydroelectric power from Canada's Nelson River available to consumers in Minnesota.

Reserve Mining Company, after a decade of legal battles, was well on the way to solving its taconite tailings disposal problem. The company was putting the finishing touches on a $370 million construction program at Milepost Seven west of Silver Bay that provided for on-land disposal of its taconite tailings. The project increased Reserve's electric demand by 28 megawatts. Minnesota Power also was in final negotiations to begin serving International Falls and its largest employer, Boise Cascade Corp.'s large wood and paper products plant. The new load totaled 35 megawatts.

The expansion of taconite production on Minnesota's Mesabi Range during the late 1960s and throughout the 1970s made Minnesota Power one of the nation's fastest-growing electric utilities during the period. Electric power demand at area taconite mills accounted for about half of the utility's kilowatt-hour sales in 1979.

The summer of 1979, in fact, was the peak of a golden era for northern Minnesota. The region's iron mining industry had undergone a renaissance in the late 1960s and 1970s, following the commercial adaptation of taconite processing. Worries in the 1950s about depleting the rich, natural ore resources of the Mesabi Range during World War II and the Korean War had been laid to rest when Erie Mining Company and Reserve Mining Company were formed in the late 1950s to mine and process taconite.

A low-grade iron ore that underlay the richer hematite formations, taconite reserves totaled several billion tons across the Mesabi and Vermilion ranges. Blasted from the earth in table-sized rocks, taconite was trucked to mills where it was crushed to the consistency of talcum powder. Bound with bentonite, a clay mined in Wyoming, and fired in kilns to nearly 3,000 degrees Fahrenheit, marble-sized taconite pellets were enriched to 65-percent iron content and rail-hauled down to Duluth, Superior, Two Harbors and Taconite Harbor. There, they were poured into the holds of lake vessels for the four-day trip down the Great Lakes to the blast furnaces of North America's integrated steel industry.

Minnesota voters in 1964 had nearly unanimously approved a constitutional amendment, called the Taconite Amendment, to restructure the way mining properties and operations were taxed. The result was a virtual explosion of taconite production on the Mesabi Iron Range between 1964 and 1979. U.S. Steel, Bethlehem Steel, Rouge Steel, Stelco, Dofasco and a half-dozen other North American integrated steel companies partnered to build taconite processing facilities in Minnesota. The steel companies and their wholly owned fleets also laid the keels for a dozen thousand-foot bulk vessels between 1968 and 1978 to haul the pellets on the Great Lakes.

The massive capital investment in northern Minnesota was made because the enriched iron pellets, in fact, were far superior to natural ore when it came to charging steel mill blast furnaces. Taconite improved productivity, conserved energy and allowed operators greater quality control of steel production from the blast furnaces.

Economically, taconite was a boon to much of northern Minnesota. In the space of 20 years, the industry grew from zero to 60 million tons of capacity by 1979. Some 15,000 steelworkers were employed in northern Minnesota, mining and refining taconite. Thousands more residents found work on the railroads, ore docks and lake vessels that moved the pellets from the Mesabi Range to steel mills. The industry spent hundreds of millions of dollars each year buying material from local suppliers, everything from giant mining tires to hard hats.

Minnesota Power's Laskin Energy Center near Hoyt Lakes, on the eastern end of the Mesabi Range, was a key component of the taconite industry's energy requirements in 1979.

Al Hodnik, who would go to work full time for Minnesota Power in 1982, was a student at the University of Minnesota in 1979 and working summers at the Laskin Energy Center to help finance his education. The son of a longtime Laskin employee, Hodnik grew up in Aurora during the growth years of the 1970s.

"And basically, it was boom times up in that neck of the woods when I grew up," Hodnik recalled years later, "with the expansion of Erie Mining Company and Reserve Mining Company and also the power plant being built. We thought we were really living in 'high cotton,' as it were, on the Iron Range at that particular time."

High cotton or good times, it was an era when anybody who wanted a job could find work. More than one Iron Ranger with an advanced degree returned to Hibbing or Virginia to work in the mill because the union pay scale at Minntac or Hibbing Taconite Company (Hibtac) was double what he or she could make teaching in Fargo or at an office job in the Twin Cities.

The other pillars of the natural resource economy of northern Minnesota, timber harvesting and tourism, also were doing well, but not as well as taconite. Timber harvesting rapidly was becoming more mechanized. Major pulp and paper producers such as Blandin, Potlatch and Boise Cascade were in the process of upgrading mill facilities at Grand Rapids, Cloquet and International Falls. Federal designation of the Voyageur's National Park on the Kabetogema Peninsula and expansion of the Boundary Waters Canoe Area in northeastern Minnesota were pumping tourism dollars into Ely, Tower-Soudan, Ranier and Orr.

But the natural resource economy of northern Minnesota has ridden a boom and bust cycle since iron ore was first discovered on the Vermilion Range in the early 1880s. And as the summer of 1979 wound down, the long boom of the 1960s and 1970s was about to go bust.

Chinks in the Armor

For northern Minnesota, the first cracks in the region's economy appeared in the late summer of 1979 when local unions of the grain millers serving the terminal elevators at the Duluth-Superior harbor walked out

The Duluth-Superior harbor maintained its ranking as North America's number one iron port during the taconite revolution of the 1960s and 1970s.

in a dispute over wages and hours. The 1970s had been good years for the Twin Ports, and a thaw in U.S.-Soviet relations had led to sharply increased exports of grain to the U.S.S.R.

The grain millers' strike, coming just as the harvest of spring wheat, durum and oats rolled into the Twin Ports aboard overflowing trucks and rail cars, could not have come at a worse time. Overnight, dozens of saltwater vessels chartered to carry grain from the head of Lake Superior to Rotterdam, southern Europe and the Soviet Black Sea ports found themselves riding at anchor in the outer harbor while management at local elevators argued with union employees.

In the end, the strike lasted nearly three months. Some grain buyers overseas vowed never again to do business with Duluth-Superior. Port officials and grain elevator executives knew that it would be a difficult task for the region to regain its reputation as one of the most efficient grain ports on the Great Lakes.

No sooner was the strike settled than international geo-politics fully disrupted the area's grain trade. In December 1979, the Soviet Union invaded Afghanistan to prop up a friendly communist dictator. In retaliation, President Jimmy Carter embargoed U.S. grain sales to the Soviets. Coming on the heels of the grain millers' strike, it was a blow from which the port would take more than a decade to recover.

"There were two or three years that were very lean, especially going from where it was just absolutely crazy," explained longtime Duluth stevedore Chuck Hilleren. In fact, grain exports through the Twin Ports peaked at nearly 10 million tons in 1980. By 1985, they had dropped to three million tons, and the average for the latter half of the 1980s was just over four million tons a year.

The Twin Ports, Minnesota Power's largest concentration of residential customers, including Superior residents served by subsidiary Superior Water, Light & Power Co., suffered further economic losses in 1979 and 1980 when the U.S. government closed the Duluth Air Force Base in the first round of Reagan-era base closings. At the same time, native son Jeno F. Paulucci closed most of his food processing facilities in Duluth, moving them to a more modern plant in southwest Ohio.

The net result was the loss of several thousand jobs in Duluth-Superior between 1979 and 1983. But the real threat to the region's economy wasn't particularly visible to area residents in 1979 and 1980. Although nobody knew it at the time, the Thanksgiving Day 1979 grounding of the Cleveland-Cliffs carrier *Frontenac* off Silver Bay was an ill omen for North America's iron and steel industry.

Restructuring American Steel

Then seemingly at the peak of its postwar prosperity, the nation's iron and steel industry was heading toward an inevitable fall in late 1979. Saddled with inefficient plants that in many cases were close to a century old and union contracts that made steelworkers the best paid industrial workers in America, iron and steel companies at the dawn of the 1980s were bleeding red ink.

Competition from imports had been increasing ever since the six-month-long United Steelworkers of America (USWA) strike against the industry in 1959. Steel "mini-mills," utilizing electric arc furnaces to melt scrap, were just beginning to take market share away from the integrated mills, especially in the low-grade segment of the market such as construction reinforcing bar.

In December 1979, U.S. Steel, the nation's largest steel firm, recognized the obvious and announced it was closing a number of its outdated and inefficient mills, most in the Monongahela River Valley south of Pittsburgh. Several of the other major steel companies, including Bethlehem Steel, J&L Steel, Armco Steel and Wheeling-Pittsburgh Steel, followed suit in 1980 and 1981. In two years' time, the steel companies put thousands of steelworkers on what in effect was permanent layoff.

By 1982, the restructuring of American steel was in full swing. Mills in the Monongahela, Mahoning and Lehigh valleys shut down their aged blast furnaces. Rolling mills that long had dominated the landscape between South Chicago and Gary, Indiana, were demolished for scrap. Thriving company towns in a dozen states—Youngstown, Ohio; Homestead and Clairton, Pennsylvania; Whiting, Indiana; Weirton, West Virginia; Lackawanna, New York—were dotted with boarded-up shops and vacant homes. Moving vans and yard sales became an increasingly common sight as a generation packed up and left the Rust Belt for greener pastures in the South and Southwest.

A telling sign came in 1982 when U.S. Steel, the world's first billion dollar corporation, purchased Marathon Oil in an effort to diversify from the steel industry. Raw steel production at USX was halved in a decade, falling from an average of 30 million tons a year in the 1971-1975 period to just over 16 million tons a year in 1981-1985.

What executives of USX and other steel companies already were calling the rationalization of the American steel industry took remarkably little time to make itself felt on the Mesabi Iron Range. Ironically, the taconite processing facilities in northern Minnesota were the newest and most efficient capital investment in the industry's steel-making arsenal.

The giant grinding mills of Mesabi Range taconite plants (above) and the Missabe Ore Docks in West Duluth (below) were two of the casualties of the restructuring of American steel in the early 1980s.

But the 60 million tons of pellets the industry in Minnesota and Michigan's Upper Peninsula produced in 1979 were way too much iron ore for the industry to consume. In its haste to convert from natural ore to taconite in the 15 years between 1964 and 1979, the industry had overbuilt capacity by a significant amount.

The Mesabi began to feel the pain of the steel cutbacks in 1982. Nationwide, steel production fell to just under 75 million tons, about 60 percent of 1981 production. U.S. Steel only made half of the steel it had produced in 1981. More revealingly, the Pittsburgh steelmaker reported it was losing $82.20 per ton for each ton of steel it shipped. The losses and layoffs at the steel mills quickly translated into major cutbacks at the taconite processing facilities.

In 1982, the Mesabi Range produced 23 million tons of pellets, less than 40 percent of the production level achieved in 1979. Minntac, U.S. Steel's flagship plant at Mountain Iron, produced only 3 million tons in 1982, 20 percent of its rated capacity of 15 million tons. U.S. Steel's Great Lakes Fleet brought out 24 vessels in April 1982 and laid up half of them

by the start of summer. The big lake fleet finished the 1982 season with a half-dozen vessels running.

For the region, the biggest and most immediate effect of the downturn in taconite processing was an unemployment level that hadn't been seen since the Great Depression. Minntac pared its work force by three-quarters from 4,200 salaried and hourly workers to slightly more than 1,000 employees by 1984. On the Iron Range, employment in the taconite industry plummeted from 16,500 workers in 1979 to barely more than 5,500 three years later. Unemployment in St. Louis County topped 20 percent in the winter of 1982-1983, and many of those laid off by the taconite plants would never get their jobs back.

The restructuring of the nation's iron and steel industry also hit suppliers to Minnesota's taconite mines and mills particularly hard. Robert S. Mars was a co-owner of W.P. & R.S. Mars Company, an area business that primarily dealt in the industrial sales of tools, conveyor belts, pullers, light machine tools and the tooling for taconite plants and paper mills. "The

As the nation's integrated steel mills on the Lower Great Lakes banked their blast furnaces in the early 1980s, fewer and fewer taconite pellets were produced on the Mesabi Range.

taconite companies had a terrible time," Mars described conditions in the early 1980s. "There were a lot of layoffs, and our business, for example, ran right alongside of all that. We were very, very low in sales and low in profit during those years. We closed some warehouses that we had on the Mesabi Range."

Mars, a World War II veteran of the U.S. Navy and a graduate of Carleton College, had been asked by President Clay C. Boswell to join the then Minnesota Power & Light Co. board of directors in 1970, following a successful stint as chairman of the Duluth School Board in the 1960s. As such, Mars had a front row seat for Minnesota Power's emergence from the wreckage of the nation's iron and steel industry.

The Value of Take-or-Pay Contracts

In 1979, almost two-thirds of Minnesota Power's nearly 9 billion kilowatt-hour (kWh) sales were to seven of the eight large taconite plants on Minnesota's Mesabi Iron Range. Half of every dollar in revenue was derived from kWh sales to the taconite industry. With Northern Indiana Public Service Company (NIPSCO), which served the blast furnaces of the steel industry in northwestern Indiana just east of Chicago, Minnesota Power shared the distinction of being one of the two most heavily industrial electric utilities in the nation.

Shareholders could have been forgiven for thinking that Minnesota Power's reliance on the taconite industry would translate into sharply lower kWh sales in the early 1980s. A short paragraph on page 8 of the Company's 1981 annual report explained why that wasn't the case. "Minnesota Power is protected from some of the economic uncertainty in the mining industry by contracts which allow the Company to recover most of its fixed costs from large customers," the paragraph read, "even if the customer shuts down or curtails production."

Internally, Minnesota Power personnel referred to the agreements with large industrial customers such as the taconite processing plants as take-or-pay contracts. It was an apt description. Under the contractual arrangements worked out with the Large Power customers, Minnesota

The Square Butte Electric Cooperative near Center, North Dakota, was a joint venture between Minnesota Power and Minnkota Power Cooperative of Grand Forks, North Dakota.

Power was paid for a certain level of electric power consumption whether the customer used it or not. Most of the take-or-pay contracts had a 10-year term, with at least one five-year renewal option.

At the time the steel industry was restructuring, the take-or-pay contracts had existed for more than 15 years. In the wake of the passage of the Taconite Amendment in 1964, Minnesota Power had begun an ambitious construction program. The take-or-pay contracts had been a requirement of the bond houses and money center banks that had provided the financing for the new construction.

During the 1970s, Minnesota Power had been one of the fastest-growing utilities in the United States. The Company had installed a 350-megawatt generator at the Clay Boswell Generating Station on the Mississippi River near Cohasset. No sooner had Boswell Unit 3 gone on line in 1973 than Minnesota Power announced that it was joining Minnkota Power Cooperative of Grand Forks, North Dakota in the formation of the Square Butte Electric Cooperative. Square Butte entailed the construction of a 438-megawatt mine-mouth generating plant in the lignite fields of North Dakota, near Center, and building an innovative, high-voltage direct current transmission line from north of Bismarck to Duluth.

By the time the Square Butte project was nearing completion, Minnesota Power was well under way with its plans for Boswell Unit 4, a 500-megawatt, low-sulfur coal-fired generator that went into commercial operation early in 1980.

Minnesota Power wheeled the electric power generated by Square Butte Electric Cooperative back to Minnesota by an innovative, direct current transmission system.

In less than a decade, Minnesota Power had built and started commercial operation of the three largest generating units in its history. The Company had added nearly 1,300 megawatts of baseload capacity to meet taconite industry demand. The financing costs had been enormous. Minnesota Power borrowed almost $900 million during the 1970s to add generating capacity to build the Energy Control Center in Duluth and to upgrade high-voltage transmission lines across northern Minnesota.

What was even more astounding about the growth was how small the Company was when it embarked upon the taconite-related expansion. In 1970, the Company's total assets were only $182 million. Consequently, when major money center banks such as Chase Manhattan and Chemical Bank of New York participated in the financing of a Square Butte Project or a Boswell expansion, they demanded assurances that Minnesota Power would be able to repay the money.

Minnesota Power had committed to its 1970s construction program because the steel companies building taconite plants on the Iron Range did not want to own and operate electric power facilities. Minnesota Power possessed the expertise to most efficiently build and run power plants. The Company also had the low-sulfur coal contracts with Peabody Coal and the Burlington Northern Railway that would help the taconite plants comply with federal and state clean air statutes. Congress had passed Clean Air legislation in the early 1970s that changed the way power plants and industrial facilities were sited and erected. In the end, Minnesota Power was simply able to run power plants more efficiently and cheaper than the steel companies could.

"I remember distinctly going to visit all these companies with Jack Rowe," reported Arend Sandbulte, who was then Minnesota Power's vice president of finance. "And he

Jack F. Rowe's engineering savvy helped Minnesota Power build some of the most efficient coal-fired generating units in the Midwest.

said, 'Before we build Boswell 3 and certainly Boswell 4, we are not going to build these plants and Square Butte unless we have take-or-pay contracts with the taconites and the paper mills, too.' They all had the option at that time of building their own power plants, but they did not do that for obvious reasons."

As conditions in the iron and steel industry deteriorated in the early 1980s, the steel companies engaged in a full-court press to withdraw from the 10-year take-or-pay contracts with Minnesota Power. The utility did what it could to renegotiate the terms of contracts, but the Company's hands were tied because of its obligations to the bankers who had financed the expansion program.

"There was a lot of complaining by the steel companies," Sandbulte said of the early 1980s. "We had many meetings with them but we always said, and everybody agreed, I think, that we could cut our throats but it was not going to make or save the national steel industry. They were losing $4 to $5 billion a year. So we would help. We constructed agreements that gave them some relief by extended contracts."

Minnesota Power also began an inevitable contraction of its own in 1980 and 1981. With Boswell Unit 4 completed, the utility in 1981 initiated a broad cost-cutting program. That year, the Company reduced the authorized work force by 103 positions. Most of the reductions were through retirements and not filling positions.

"One of the concerns I've had during our period of tremendous growth over the past several years," Chairman and President Jack F. Rowe told employees in an early 1980 interview, "is that we don't want to get in the situation of hiring too many people and then having to resort to wholesale cutbacks and layoffs."

The Architect of Expansion

Jack F. Rowe was an engineer's engineer. He lived most of his life in northern Minnesota and helped the Company he joined in 1950 become one of the best-run utilities in North America. Before he retired as Minnesota Power's president, chairman and chief executive officer in 1988, Jack Rowe had presided over the transformation of the Company he headed for much of the 1970s and 1980s.

Bob Mars, who served on the board of directors for all of Rowe's tenure at the helm of Minnesota Power, recalled a man who kept a firm hand on the reins. "Jack was a very dedicated guy to his job," Mars said. "He was an engineer, and he had grown up through the Company."

Mars also remembered a utility CEO who was never hesitant to get out of the office. "Jack was a committed sportsman," Mars said. "He enjoyed Minnesota's outdoors and got his relaxation doing a little fishing and hunting, and I did a little of that with him."

Born in Sebeka in 1927, Rowe spent his early years in the northern Minnesota logging community of Littlefork before moving with his family to Duluth in the early 1940s. Rowe graduated from Duluth Denfeld High School in 1945, served in the U.S. Navy immediately after World War II and returned to the Twin Ports in 1946 to attend Duluth Junior College. He earned his B.S. degree in electrical engineering at the University of Minnesota in 1950 and again returned to Duluth when M.L. Hibbard offered him a job at Minnesota Power.

For most of the 1950s, Rowe worked in the Company's general engineering department under the legendary Hubbell Carpenter. He helped plan Boswell Units 1 and 2 in the mid-1950s, and worked with the crews building a 115,000-volt backbone transmission line up the North Shore of Lake Superior in the late 1950s. Rowe succeeded Carpenter as chief engineer in 1963.

Axel Herbert had been named president of Minnesota Power in 1962. The genial Herbert had spent his entire career in sales and marketing. In 1966, Clay Boswell called Rowe into his office. Boswell told Rowe that he felt "Axel needed some technical support to review things that would come from other departments of the Company." Boswell, the chairman of the Company's board of directors, asked Rowe if he would serve as Herbert's assistant. Rowe agreed, and he was named a vice president in 1967. Two years later, in 1969, he was promoted to executive vice president and named to the board of directors.

In 1973, at the time that crews were completing Boswell Unit 3 and doing the detailed planning for Boswell Unit 4 and Square Butte Electric

Cooperative, Rowe was named chief operating officer. During the next decade, Rowe presided over the first transformation of the Company, from a sleepy northern Minnesota utility to a key component in the natural resources development of the Lake Superior region.

"The whole tenor of the Company changed," Rowe told an interviewer

For much of the 1960s and 1970s, Minnesota Power was in the construction business.

in 1983. "We had a major hiring program. We had a major expansion program. We hired a large number of engineers and technical people, and we got into the 20th century in the area of computers and sophisticated equipment."

Two years after Rowe was named president of Minnesota Power in 1978, America's iron and steel industry began the painful process of restructuring that saw employment slashed by two-thirds in the Mesabi Range taconite industry. In 1980, Rowe set in motion a slimming down at Minnesota Power to meet his goal of not passing along rate increases to customers until at least 1987. After 1983, he would preside over the second transformation of Minnesota Power that would result in the Duluth utility becoming one of the most diversified electric power producers in the United States by 1990.

Jack F. Rowe retired in 1988, splitting his time during the next 16 years between his summer home at Schultz Lake and his winter residence in Naples, Florida. Rowe died in Duluth on April 8, 2005, following a lengthy illness. He was followed within weeks by the death of Mary, his beloved wife of 49 years.

Jack Rowe's stamp on Minnesota Power was in some ways more pronounced than that of his engineering predecessors, Clay Boswell and M.L. Hibbard. With his work on Boswell Units 3 and 4 during the 1970s, Rowe proved himself easily the equal of Boswell and Hibbard as a builder and engineer. But it was Rowe's leadership in engineering the cultural transformation of Minnesota Power through its diversification initiatives during the 1980s that is his legacy to the company he loved.

CHAPTER 3 The Diversification Imperative

By 1983, it was becoming increasingly clear to executives at Minnesota Power that the troubles affecting the iron and steel industry were more than a typical recession. 1982 was a dismal year for the Mesabi Range. 1983 was little better. Pellet production topped out at 25 million tons—slightly higher than the 1982 low of 23 million tons—but still less than half of the tonnage produced in 1979.

The entire North American iron ore industry was in free fall during the mid-1980s. Capacity was shaved by nearly 40 percent between 1982 and 1985, with numerous iron ore mines in California, Wyoming, Michigan and Wisconsin closed forever during the period. Iron ore and pellet plants would permanently shutter 35 million tons of capacity in just five years.

On the steel mill side of the ledger, names that were legendary in American industrial production were being shut down, their furnaces idled, their work force dispersed. In December 1983, David Roderick, the chairman of U.S. Steel Corp., announced the closure of American Bridge, once the largest structural steel fabricating plant in the world.

What was even more troubling for Minnesota Power executives and Minnesota policymakers was the fact that Mesabi Range taconite plants were not competitive with iron ore mines elsewhere in the world. In 1983, several steel companies experimented with importing Brazilian iron ore to Chicago. What they discovered caused jaws to drop from Pittsburgh to Duluth.

Companhe Val Rio Doce (CVRD), the big Brazilian iron ore producer, was able to land iron concentrate in Chicago at $38 per long ton. CVRD operated some of the richest natural ore mines in the world. Most of its iron ore in the early 1980s was ocean-shipped to steel mills in Japan and Europe. The experimental shipments to Chicago utilized the St. Lawrence Seaway, which was constrained by draft limitations that wouldn't allow the Brazilian ore the same cost advantages it enjoyed in deeper draft ports in Europe and Japan.

But even at the shipping disadvantage, Brazilian ore landed in Chicago at a significant discount to ore from Minnesota. The three most efficient Mesabi Range mines landed pellets in Chicago at $45 per long ton.

"In the 1982 to 1986 years, foreign pellets were a real threat," Dr. Peter Kakela wrote. Kakela, professor of resource development at Michigan State University, is one of the world's experts in the iron ore trade. "Foreign pellets could be delivered to lower lake ports for less than what it cost to produce and deliver pellets from the best mines in Minnesota," Kakela noted. "In addition, the advent of the U.S. spot market in 1982 made the traditional pricing practices, as well as high costs, untenable."

In 1982 and 1983, the message went out from Pittsburgh, Chicago, Cleveland and other centers of the nation's iron and steel industry to the taconite processing plants of the Lake Superior country: Cut costs and increase productivity, or close.

Minnesota Power already had demonstrated a commitment to cutting costs in the early 1980s with aggressive initiatives to control operations and maintenance costs and an accelerated early retirement program. Construction expenditures were more than halved between 1980 and 1982 to $32 million, and fuel and purchased power costs dropped $17 million to $125 million in the same period. The reduction in the work force, accomplished almost entirely through retirements and not filling vacant positions, reduced the Company's employment levels by more than 15 percent between 1980 and 1985.

The success of the cost control programs in the early 1980s allowed Minnesota Power to pledge to its customers not to raise rates for the remainder of the 1980s. In late 1982, the Company made a proposal to all of its taconite customers to reduce contract charges for five years by an aggregate $8 million per year. In return, the taconite firms would agree to extend their contracts by one year. Six of the Company's seven taconite customers accepted the offer. Two of the companies rescinded their previous cancellations of contracts.

The cost controls Minnesota Power implemented in 1980 began paying dividends by mid-decade. In 1983, Minnesota Power's taconite customers paid an average of 5.19 cents per kilowatt-hour for electricity. By 1989, that average had dropped to an average of 3.84 cents per kilowatt-hour, a 35-percent reduction.

A Sometimes Adversarial Relationship

The 1982 extension agreements with the Company's taconite customers aside, the early 1980s were an extraordinarily stressful period for Minnesota Power executives and managers. U.S. Steel, the owner of Minntac and the utility's single biggest customer, did not participate in the 1982 extension agreement. The Pittsburgh steelmaker had gone to the Minnesota Public Utility Commission in 1981 to complain about Minnesota Power's demand charges. As a result, a fair amount of acrimony existed in the early 1980s between Minnesota Power and its largest industrial customer.

Al Harmon had a front row seat for some of that animosity. A Hoosier and a graduate of the prestigious Rose Hulman Institute of Technology in Terre Haute, Indiana, Harmon had answered an advertisement placed by Minnesota Power in late 1978 for electrical engineers. Harmon was intrigued by the change of scenery and as a result, "made the trek up here before Thanksgiving, was offered a job, came back, and got a house. I drove my wife, dog and cat, and plants and all of our worldly possessions in two vehicles in time to get to Duluth before the January freeze. We parked one vehicle in the garage of our new home and parked the other one outside. It didn't start again until sometime in March. We wondered just what we had come to."

Harmon went to work at the Herbert Service Center as an industrial service engineer. Two years later, he moved downtown to 30 West Superior Street and "became a point person with the taconites at the operating plant level." During the next several years, Harmon would be "peripherally involved with high-level taconite rate negotiations."

Harmon's boss and the Minnesota Power contact person for the taconite companies in 1982 was Al Seckinger, a tough industrial engineer whose crew cut signaled to the world his status as an ex-Marine.

Harmon recalled a meeting with Cliff Niemi, the general manager at Minntac, and other representatives of U.S. Steel during the 1982 contract extension negotiations. "As a part of showing proper respect to a very important customer," Harmon explained, "Jack Rowe came to sit in on that part of the meeting."

Rowe, Seckinger and Harmon listened to Niemi's presentation about U.S. Steel's situation and its proposals for Minnesota Power concessions. About 11 a.m., the U.S. Steel representatives excused themselves to make a call to Pittsburgh. The three Minnesota Power representatives went outside the executive offices' conference room to discuss the proposals that had been made.

"At that point we were not prepared to make any concessions," Harmon explained. During the break, Rowe explained that he had a luncheon date. Rowe said he would go back into the meeting for 10 minutes and express his displeasure with Niemi about the pace of the negotiations before excusing himself.

After Rowe left the meeting, Seckinger and Harmon continued to negotiate. "We did wind up finding ways to address their issues while not giving away the store," Harmon said. "But that was kind of the way things started. We always had to be sure that they knew we were dealing from a position of strength. They weren't going to just roll over this little electric Company."

Taconite company complaints had a tendency to end up in the public arena. Iron Range native Rudy Perpich, who had been governor of Minnesota for a short time in the mid-1970s, recaptured the governor's office in the November 1982 election. The balance of power in the Minnesota Legislature was held by the Iron Range delegation, which was solidly Democrat Farmer Labor (DFL) and extremely sensitive to the economic woes suffered by constituents in northern Minnesota. If a taconite customer complained to the Minnesota Public Utilities Commission (MPUC) about its electric rates, the complaint was sure to appear on the front pages of the state's newspapers.

The problems afflicting Minnesota Power's taconite customers created an internal debate at the Company over the future of the iron and steel industry. As early as 1981, employees began to discuss the wisdom of being an energy supplier captive to the taconite industry. Some in the utility pointed out that Minnesota Power essentially had been a construction management firm during the 1970s when it built Boswell Units 3 and 4 and the Square Butte project. Others questioned the advisability of placing all of Minnesota Power's eggs in the taconite basket. In any case, informal discussions about the future of Minnesota Power were increasingly common by 1982.

Internal debates about the utility's dependence on the taconite industry for its continued growth were brought into sharp focus three years later when the first of a depressing litany of bankruptcies washed over the steel industry. Wheeling-Pittsburgh Steel Co., one of the 10 largest steelmakers in the nation, filed for Chapter 11 protection in the spring of 1985. In the summer of 1986, LTV Steel Corp. became the second major steel manufacturer to file bankruptcy. Once a company's affairs were in the hands of a bankruptcy trustee, contracts theoretically could be invalidated by the trustee, a possibility that posed very negative implications for Minnesota Power's take-or-pay contracts.

Bankruptcy of steel companies was something that Jack Rowe was certainly aware of as early as the 1982-1983 period. In the summer of 1982, he sat down with the editor of *Contact*, the monthly employee newspaper, to discuss a range of issues. One was the deteriorating condition of the region's taconite producers.

"We depend on the taconite industry for half our revenue," Rowe told employees, "so what happens to American steelmakers is of great concern to us. In an extreme case—and this is just hypothetical—if a steel company was to go into receivership or something like that, it would hurt us. The domestic steel manufacturers own Minnesota's taconite plants, and Minnesota Power's contracts with taconite customers are only as good as the credit of the companies who signed them."

Rowe went on to emphasize that Minnesota Power did not know of "any imminent problems with the solvency of any particular firm, but obviously steel companies can't continue to lose money as they have this year."

A Flexible Corporate Response

In the August 1982 interview with *Contact*, Rowe began to outline a flexible corporate response to Minnesota Power's predicament that had been in the development stage for the previous two years. "It would, of course, be an advantage to reduce our heavy dependence on one major industry," Rowe said.

One way to reduce that dependence, he added, was through diversification. "We won't be expanding our electric system facilities much in the coming years, and some outside growth prospects might be beneficial and stimulating. Diversification would create opportunities for employees. If we can build on expertise we have and use our facilities more effectively, that would benefit our shareholders and customers as well."

Although the discussion about diversification was the first many of the utility's 1,450 employees had heard of the strategy, Minnesota Power was already well on the way to implementing policies that would free it from its "dependence on one major industry."

Utility executives had begun to investigate diversification in 1980. By 1981, they proposed an amendment to Minnesota Power's charter to allow the Company to pursue general business purposes. Jack Rowe told shareholders at the 1981 annual meeting that the Company had no specific plans for diversification at the time, but "if we do decide to diversify, it would most likely be in an energy-related area. Be assured that we will look very carefully at any diversification activity before proceeding."

Following shareholder approval of the amendment, Minnesota Power moved ahead that summer with the formation of the Strategic Investigations Group (SIG). Initially a small task force, SIG was headed by Jack McDonald. A Duluth native with a B.S. degree in physics, McDonald joined Minnesota Power during the 1970s and worked in operations analysis and budgeting before being named the Company's director of materials management in the late 1970s.

McDonald and his assistant, Scott Vierima, used much of 1981 and 1982 to investigate the success of other electric utilities that had already diversified from power production. They analyzed Pacific Power & Light Company, then the seventh largest coal operator in the nation and the manager of a telephone satellite system in Alaska. They studied the operations of Gulf States Utilities and its gas development subsidiary. Closer to home, McDonald and Vierima took a close look at Montana-Dakota Utilities (MDU) in Bismarck, North Dakota. By 1980, MDU was deriving 25 percent of its annual revenues from lignite coal mining in North Dakota and oil production on the Cedar Creek Anticline of Montana and Wyoming.

McDonald and Vierima, who reported to Executive Vice President Arend Sandbulte, also spent a fair amount of time in 1981 in internal discussions with James Habicht of the Minnesota Power legal staff. Habicht was the Company's primary liaison with the MPUC, which had been established by the Minnesota Legislature just seven years before, in 1974.

There were a number of questions about how diversified activity would be treated by regulatory bodies, both in Minnesota and nationwide. Dr. Terry Farrar, a staff member at the Edison Electric Institute (EEI), told *The New York Times* in the spring of 1981 that "in some states, (utility) commissions are inclined to look at the profits of an unregulated subsidiary and include it in the calculations either explicitly or implicitly when determining rate structure. And that's a significant disincentive to diversify."

In a roundtable discussion published by the prestigious *Public Utilities Fortnightly* that spring, Lelan F. Sillin Jr., the president and CEO of Northeast Utilities, summarized the issue. "At the state level," Sillin said, "utilities must be assured that profits arising from investments by shareholders in competitive, risk-laden activities will flow to the shareholders and will not be used to subsidize electric energy rates for consumers."

In September 1981, Minnesota Power hired economics consultant Irwin Stelzer to travel to Duluth to brief the utility's managers. Stelzer, the president of National Economic Research Associates, then one of the most respected utility consulting firms in North America, was an unabashed supporter of utility diversification efforts. Waving an unlit eight-inch cigar to emphasize his point, Stelzer told Company management that "managers of electric utilities are schizophrenics. They don't know if they work for the shareholder or the customer."

Stelzer painted a bleak regulatory picture. With interest rates at the time at 14 percent or more, and Minnesota Power unable to earn a rate of return that would bring its common shares above book value, the Company faced difficulties well beyond the problems affecting the Company's taconite customers.

Stelzer suggested that Minnesota Power might best be served by embarking on a limited program of diversification. But he cautioned that diversification was rife with pitfalls, including the need to adapt to a competitive marketplace and the danger that utility commissions would confuse diversification with diversion of cash from utility customers.

"If you're going to have a diversification program," Stelzer told Minnesota Power managers, "work out the nitty-gritty problems with the Public Utilities Commission beforehand."

Habicht was able to assure Sandbulte and McDonald that the MPUC likely would not reject the idea of diversification without at least considering the matter, and Minnesota Power elected to take its initiatives one step further. During the fall of 1981 and spring of 1982, McDonald and Vierima contacted investment bankers, business brokers and the management of other utilities either involved in or contemplating diversification activities. By the spring of 1982, McDonald, who had been named director of corporate diversification studies in late 1981, and SIG had concluded that Minnesota Power possessed the strengths to at least contemplate taking diversification activities to a more formal level of Company participation.

McDonald told management that he sensed that Minnesota Power was able to adapt to and effectively use new technology; that the Company was financially innovative and comfortable working within a regulatory framework; and that Minnesota Power was at ease working with the public.

In the summer of 1982, McDonald suggested that Minnesota Power suspend diversification activities until he and his staff could complete a long-range strategic diversification plan. To do that, McDonald recommended entering into a contractual agreement with Power Technologies, a Schenectady, New York, consulting firm.

McDonald also advised that SIG be upgraded to a formal task force with the addition of Donnie Crandell, an analyst from the corporate diversification department, and Roberta Grube of the planning department. Also joining the task force were analysts Don Stellmaker and Chuck Pleski, as well as Dave Gartzke for his financial expertise.

"Power Technologies will give us computer models," McDonald told Sandbulte. "The strategic goals we are going to have to give ourselves. The people who develop them are the people who are going to have to execute them."

The report that recommended the utility continue with the development of a full-blown corporate diversification strategy called for a second stage effort to begin evaluating specific business opportunities outside the electric utility business. Some of those opportunities, McDonald said, would come from business activities that Minnesota Power was already starting to pursue.

McDonald's report was issued at what was perhaps the nadir of taconite's fortunes during the 1980s restructuring of the iron and steel industry. In the summer of 1982, Eveleth Mines was the only taconite firm operating on the Mesabi Range, and it was on a sharply reduced, four-day-week schedule. Reserve and Minntac were shut down from June through the remainder of the year. Inland Steel Mining Company, Butler Taconite and National Steel Pellet had extended their summer shutdowns through September, while Hibtac began a 10-week layoff on July 4.

The Topeka Group

The elevation of the SIG effort to task force status had more significance for most Minnesota Power personnel than a mere name change. Company employees were already quite familiar with task forces. In what would presage the Company's major commitment to an innovative organizational development initiative in the mid- and late 1980s, Minnesota Power embarked upon a series of task forces in 1980 and 1981 to address personnel and human resources issues.

Task Forces on Effectiveness, Paperwork Reduction, Recognition, Employee Benefits, Training and Development, and Compensation gave the Company's young managers a chance to tackle work force concerns in a collegial atmosphere. The exercise also firmly identified the importance of task forces for the Company's salaried and hourly employees.

By 1984, Minnesota Power was pledging to shareholders that it planned to derive 25 percent of Company earnings from diversification by the early 1990s.

The elevation of the diversification effort to task force status was a signal of the importance Minnesota Power attributed to the initiative. Diversification took another giant leap forward in December 1982 when executive management hammered out a corporate strategic plan at a two-day retreat at Quadna Mountain Resort near Hill City. Spearheaded by Gerald B. "Jerry" Ostroski, the recently named vice president for information and planning, the strategic plan envisioned two corporate goals. Minnesota Power would continue to pursue a course of moderate utility growth, while diversifying by engaging in functionally related businesses that would draw on the skills of existing employees.

Ostroski was an electrical engineer with two decades of utility experience in 1983. A native of Schofield, Wisconsin, Ostroski joined Minnesota Power in 1963, the summer he graduated from the University of Wisconsin. He worked with Bob Marchetti in the Company's planning section from 1963 to 1967, spent the next four years as a computer planning engineer, and was a transmission planning engineer from 1971 to 1975. That year, he was appointed manager of systems planning before being promoted to director of the planning department in 1978. In 1982, he was named vice president for information and planning.

One functionally related business that Minnesota Power investigated for diversification opportunities involved cabling the Upper Midwest with a fiber optics network.

During his nearly 20 years as a utility planner, Ostroski had seen the very nature of the discipline change radically. "In the earliest days," he said, "planning was mainly directed toward making sure the distribution system was capable of handling the growing loads, and the transmission system was capable of handling the growing system."

Ostroski noted that planners in the 1960s ensured "there was enough generation around, and you kind of worked with your neighbors. People would put in a generator here, and then you'd buy from your neighbor somewhere. And then they'd buy from you, and you put a generator in. So it was mostly hardware-oriented."

After Boswell 4 came on line, Ostroski continued, "we ended up not needing any or very much new hardware, and the planning also morphed from technical stuff to business planning and financial and corporate planning. All of a sudden, we were deciding how you were going to make the most money for your shareholders as opposed to just keeping the lights on. So we added the profitability aspect into the planning process, and the Company developed its financial planning models. All of those things changed from strictly hardware to more business-oriented processes, more survivability of the corporation-oriented."

With a corporate strategic plan in place, Jack Rowe was ready to announce to shareholders and the investment community that the Company was no longer going to be simply an electric utility serving the natural resources economy of northeastern Minnesota. "The fundamentals of our strategic plan are that the electric utility business will be our core business," Rowe told shareholders at the 1983 annual meeting, "but that we will expand as appropriate into related businesses in which we have gained capability through our electric utility operations."

By the time Rowe made his announcement at the St. Louis County Heritage and Arts Center in Duluth, Minnesota Power had committed to carrying forward the work it had done during the nearly three years it had invested in planning for diversification. In March 1983, two months before the annual meeting, Rowe had signed incorporation papers for Topeka Group, Inc., a utility subsidiary responsible for planning and managing Minnesota Power's diversification efforts.

Appointed to head Topeka Group—the name came from an early land and real estate subsidiary of MP&L—was Jack McDonald, the Company's longtime diversification executive. Joining him in the formal approach to diversification activities were Vierima and Crandell, as well as Dennis Fink, whose primary responsibility would be conducting marketing studies for the new subsidiary.

McDonald had ambitious goals for the new company. By 1988, he hoped to have "at least two very sizable stand-alone profit centers. When I say stand-alone, I mean that they're not particularly dependent on their parent for the basic functions that a business needs to operate."

Longer term, McDonald's goal was breathtaking, to say the least. By 1992-1993, McDonald said, "It's our objective to be providing 25 percent of the Company's earnings from the diversified activities, and by that time it should be a pretty well-established enterprise in its own right."

Minnesota Power's earnings in 1982 had been in excess of $41 million. Given a modest growth rate of 10 percent a year—the year-to-year growth from 1981 to 1982 was 17 percent—Minnesota Power's earnings could be $106 million or more in 1992. At 25 percent, Topeka Group would be reporting earnings of $26.5 million in 1992, if McDonald's ambitious goals were to be met.

McDonald was optimistic about Topeka Group's ability to make diversification happen. "I think that Minnesota Power is looking at the future," he said in the spring of 1983. "We see that the electric utility industry is maturing and feel that our Company has the basic prerequisites necessary to mount a diversification program."

Work was underway to diversify Minnesota Power into telecommunications ventures. Ostroski had been laboring for several years to develop Company expertise in threading fiber optics cable through high-voltage transmission conduit. That expertise would lead Topeka Group into its first diversification ventures, with investments in JayEn, a Duluth-based telecommunications firm, and NorLight, a consortium

Minnesota Power experimented with threading fiber optics cable through high-voltage transmission wires.

planning a fiber optics right-of-way between the Twin Cities and Chicago.

And JayEn and NorLight were only the beginning.

CHAPTER 4

From Wisconsin to Florida

With a diversification strategy firmly in place, Topeka Group set about decreasing Minnesota Power's dependence upon large industrial customers in the natural resources industry for the lion's share of its revenues. Formed in 1983, the Company's diversification subsidiary had $60 million in cash to invest and was ready to make the first major foray into non-electric utility investments in the summer of 1984.

Minnesota Power engineers understood the utility infrastructure of diversification initiatives such as JayEn and NorLight.

Earlier that year, Topeka Group had signaled its intent to diversify into telecommunications when it acquired control of JayEn, a Hermantown-based pioneer in what was then called the mobile telephone business. JayEn was small, with well under $1 million a year in revenues, but the firm was in a growing telecommunications field that Minnesota Power, with its technology expertise, was comfortable managing.

JayEn had been founded in the early 1960s by Joe Nehring, a communications technician with the Duluth, Missabe & Iron Range Railway (DM&IR), who had a sideline business selling and maintaining two-way radios. Nehring, whose nickname was J.N., used a phonetic spelling of his nickname when he incorporated JayEn, Inc. Nehring teamed with Tom Zauhar, a technician for Duluth radio and television broadcaster KDAL. The two soon began selling and servicing mobile telephone systems across northeastern Minnesota, northwestern Wisconsin and into the Upper Peninsula of Michigan.

Mobile telephone systems were bulky, battery-powered and prone to interference from airborne radar and microwave towers, but they were the predecessors of cell phone technology. When Topeka Group invested in JayEn, the Hermantown company was in the process of expanding its sales and service facilities to St. Cloud and to Fargo, North Dakota.

McDonald told directors of Minnesota Power that Topeka Group liked JayEn for its potential. "The investment in JayEn is consistent with our goal of getting into businesses that enable us to take advantage of the resource most available to us, the talent and expertise of those already employed by either Topeka Group or Minnesota Power," McDonald said. "Our decision to become involved with JayEn resulted from a cooperative research effort in which JayEn's people and ours determined that the firm has only begun to realize its potential for expansion."

One of JayEn's former partners was actually running the business, and it was experiencing financial challenges. "At that time," Don Shippar recalled, "one of my mentors, Bob Marchetti, approached me and said, 'Don, we need you to go up and run this company. You know about telecommunications.'"

Shippar told Marchetti he knew about telecommunications from the technical standpoint but that running a telecommunications company was different than running an operations and maintenance organization. "Well, Bob was a very persuasive person," Shippar recalled. "I remember Bob telling me that when the train comes by the stop, you either get on it or you get passed by. I thought about that for a minute and thought, 'That's an interesting message. There's obviously some motivation there he meant to be included in his message.' And I took up Bob's offer and said, 'Sure, why not?'"

Shippar took over responsibility for JayEn in early January 1985. "JayEn at that time was on the verge of investing in a large trunking system," Shippar said. Trunking was a predecessor to cell phone technology in that a telecommunications company would use conventional two-way radio technology and boost it long distances through the use of trunking towers.

"In essence, you'd long-haul the communication from one tower to the other so you could drive down a freeway transmitting," Shippar explained. "As you got out of the local zone or node, then when you picked up the next trunk you could transmit again. That was one of the things that was really being touted. Actually, we never made the investment, which was a good thing. And then shortly after that, we became, in essence, representatives for cellular telephone companies. We installed systems in vehicles, sold and serviced cellular systems."

Ultimately, the Topeka Group investment in JayEn didn't provide the returns that Minnesota Power expected of the diversification efforts. Folding the JayEn structure into Topeka Group left the acquired company in a 40-percent tax bracket. Coupled with overhead costs that consumed 25 percent of revenues, JayEn was too small to contribute meaningfully to Topeka Group's bottom line.

In 1986, Topeka Group sold JayEn back to one of the original partners, who still operates the company 20 years later. Shippar, a Superior native whose Minnesota Power career began in the late 1970s, returned to Minnesota Power's human resources department, where he handled labor relations for the electric utility. While it wasn't the kind of fit that characterized some of the Company's later diversification acquisitions, JayEn was a valuable testing ground for integrating diversification strategies.

UTI

No sooner was the ink dry on Minnesota Power's agreement to purchase JayEn than Topeka Group announced its first major acquisition. On June 15, 1984, Minnesota Power exercised an option to acquire Universal Telephone, Inc. (UTI), a Milwaukee-based holding company for rural telephone systems, water and wastewater treatment facilities, and manufacturing operations.

UTI was the creation of Ray Dittmore, a Wisconsin native who in 1946 had returned from World War II to start manufacturing communications equipment for the U.S. Navy and navigation and radio equipment for the U.S. Army in his Milwaukee garage.

Dittmore was the classic entrepreneur who had built from scratch a $27 million telecommunications system serving more than 42,000 customers in little more than a third of a century. Along the way, he had concentrated on acquiring rural telephone systems, which in 1984 accounted for 75 percent of UTI's revenues. Most of those systems were located in Dittmore's home state of Wisconsin. UTI operated rural telephone systems in Forestville, Winchester, Frederic, Sparta and Manitowish Waters, Wisconsin.

Dittmore's interest in Native American culture had led him to invest in telecommunications systems far afield from the Badger State. During the 1960s and 1970s, Dittmore had acquired rural telephone systems in Oklahoma and southwest Colorado, as well as on the Hopi Reservation in Arizona and on the Zuni and Pecos pueblos in New Mexico. The Universal Telephone Company of the Southwest at Keams Canyon, Arizona served customers at some of the oldest continuously inhabited communities in North America. Topeka Group staffers often commented about the anomaly of having dinner with bankers atop a skyscraper in Phoenix and meeting with Hopi elders at Mishnogovi the next day.

UTI microwave towers relayed signals across vast swaths of the American Southwest.

Dittmore's other investments were perhaps more diversified than Topeka Group was ready to tackle in 1984. The Dittmore-Freimuth Corp. was still involved in Ray Dittmore's original line of business, making electrical, communications, navigation and radio equipment for the nation's military forces. Carter Company, another subsidiary, manufactured precision machining equipment at several factories in Hawaii. Honomach Inc., a subsidiary of Carter Company, manufactured sophisticated fruit-processing equipment used by pineapple processors all over the world.

In 1983, Dittmore had formed Brown Equipment Corp. to manufacture a line of trenchers and backhoes used primarily in installing telecommunications cable.

The final piece of the Dittmore empire, which totaled almost $80 million in assets, was Southern States Utilities (SSU). The growth of Florida in the 1960s and 1970s had been predicated on the siting of planned unit developments that were commonly built in rural areas. Developers typically

UTI telephone towers stood sentinel across much of the arid Southwest, offering residents of the Hopi and Zuni Indian Reservations access to the convenience of contemporary telecommunications.

Minnesota Power initially contemplated selling UTI's Florida water and wastewater treatment operations, but growth in the business caused the Duluth utility to take a second look.

installed water and wastewater treatment systems to serve the residents of the new community and then sold the utilities to municipalities or private operators once the development had been built out.

Dittmore started purchasing water and wastewater systems in fast-growing areas of central and northeast Florida. By 1984, SSU operated 53 water and 14 wastewater utilities in Seminole, Lake, Polk, Citrus, Orange, Osceola, Putnam, Duval and Martin counties, Florida.

Topeka Group's purchase of UTI was a straight stock transaction in which Minnesota Power acquired all of Dittmore's common and preferred shares for $12 million. The purchase gave Topeka Group control of 56 percent of the company's shares. A month later, Minnesota Power made a tender offer for the $7.9 million in shares it did not control.

Topeka Group quickly sold UTI's manufacturing subsidiaries and contemplated selling SSU. But opportunities in the Florida water and wastewater treatment business continued to present themselves. In 1985, SSU purchased another seven water and wastewater treatment plants in Florida. By that time, Topeka Group also was in negotiations to buy a major stake in Deltona Corp. and its water and wastewater utilities in the Sunshine State.

UTI gave Topeka Group the critical mass to propel Minnesota Power toward the ambitious diversification goals that Jack Rowe had set for the Duluth utility. Jack McDonald, the Duluth native who headed Topeka

Group, and Donnie Crandell, his chief analyst, spent an increasing amount of time inspecting proposed acquisitions for Minnesota Power. Crandell, in particular, became a familiar figure in SSU's Apopka, Florida, office, using the growing water utility as a base of operations for his buying forays across the Southeast.

Minnesota Power began transferring talented people from Duluth to the far-flung subsidiary operation. When Chuck Wood, Minnesota Power's director of human resources, transferred to a similar job with SSU in 1986, it became evident to most employees that diversification was going to be the wave of the Company's future.

By 1986, Minnesota Power also was involved with its largest diversification project, a greenfield paper mill that would transform West Duluth.

CHAPTER 5 Strengthening the Base

O ne of the traditional activities engaged in by electric utilities nationwide has been economic development. Utilities long have realized that the economic health of the communities they serve is key to electric power sales. As early as the 1930s, MP&L's area development department supported new and emerging industries in the utility's service territory with cash incentives, introductory power rates and in-kind expertise. Area development specialists worked with municipal officials, small business owners and northern Minnesota farmers to use electricity as efficiently as possible.

M.L. Hibbard had first established MP&L's area development department during the Great Depression. In the late 1940s and early 1950s, Howard Cooper earned the utility a much-deserved reputation for competence with his work in area development.

The long period of prosperity from the 1950s to the beginning of the 1980s, coupled with economies of scale that resulted in steadily declining electric power rates for much of that period, led Minnesota Power to de-emphasize the Company's traditional role in area development activities. After 1973, when rate increases to pay for construction of Boswell Units 3 and 4 and the Square Butte project reversed the declining cost of electricity in northern Minnesota, some critics charged that activities such as area development only added to electricity's costs in the region.

That all changed after 1982 with the implosion of the taconite economy. Suddenly, economic development became a rallying cry for residents of northeastern Minnesota. Incoming Governor Rudy Perpich and the DFL Iron Range delegation in the Minnesota Legislature began encouraging investment in local businesses that could help diversify the region's iron and steel economy.

Existing economic development organizations, such as the Iron Range Resources and Rehabilitation Board (IRRRB), the Northeastern Minnesota Development Association (NEMDA) and the Seaway Port Authority of Duluth (SPAD), ramped up staff and resources to encourage economic development in the area.

Some of the early effort was scattershot and duplicated. To help coordinate the effort, Jack Rowe in late 1982 called a meeting of vice presidents, directors and department heads to discuss what Minnesota Power could do to assist. An outgrowth of the meeting was the creation of a task force that would investigate Minnesota Power's role in economic development for northeastern Minnesota.

Named to the Economic Development Task Force were Vice Presidents Arend Sandbulte, Bob Marchetti, Bob Miller, Ray Erickson and Jerry Ostroski. Also named were Al Seckinger and Al Harmon from energy services, Donnie Crandell and Dennis Fink from Topeka Group, and Jim Roberts from Public Affairs.

The task force members quickly concluded that Minnesota Power could best utilize its resources by concentrating on three areas. The Company could compile economic data to be available for use by all development groups in the region. Minnesota Power would attempt to help out existing manufacturers in the service territory and would begin a quiet campaign of contacting prime candidates for locating in northeastern Minnesota. It was the latter goal that would lead to the Company's biggest economic development success.

By the spring of 1983, the task force reported its conclusions to Jack Rowe: Minnesota Power should establish a formal economic development department. Rowe located the unit in the offices of Minnesota Power's public affairs department, reporting to Vice President Ray Erickson.

The director Rowe named to head the economic development department was a 35-year veteran employee then on loan to a Duluth-based economic development organization. C.T. "Bud" Sickel had joined the Company's engineering department in 1948. From 1962 to 1980, Sickel had served as general manager of the Company's Northern Division. In 1981, he had been a special assistant to Jack Rowe, and in 1982, was loaned to NEMDA to head its Duluth New Business Cooperation Office.

Sickel told *Contact* in a late 1983 interview that his experience would lend itself well to the new position. "I'm aware of what's going on out in our divisions where most of the economic development groups are now organized," Sickel said. "And I know how they operate within our divisional set-up. I know that these groups have been active in the past. They are now getting active again."

One thing Minnesota Power's economic development efforts would not do, Sickel said, was "to try and direct those groups. We are going to attempt to provide leadership assistance to these groups and to help them whenever we can."

Another pitfall Minnesota Power would attempt to avoid at all costs was to play favorites when it came to economic development incentives. Sickel noted that Minnesota Power "would like to see some economic development on the Iron Range and in Duluth, but not at the expense of some other area. If in fact somebody would want to move into the Park

Rapids, Walker or Little Falls area, we would be all for it. I can't visualize a situation where we would help to switch them to another location in the service territory."

Through late 1983 and early 1984, Sickel worked at prioritizing a number of different tasks for the new economic development efforts. Jack Rowe and Minnesota Power's executive team had set a number of ambitious goals for the department, including benchmarking Minnesota Power against other utilities, creating assistance packages for existing businesses, identifying existing companies for assistance and analyzing possible candidates for relocation.

While Sickel was dealing with growing pains in the economic development department, Minnesota Power quietly was putting together one of the largest economic development projects in northeastern Minnesota since the heyday of the taconite construction era more than a decade before.

The Origins of LSPI

Minnesota Power's involvement with the construction and eventual ownership of Lake Superior Paper Industries (LSPI) originated in the

Lake Superior Paper Industries was the first greenfield paper mill built in Minnesota since early in the 20th century.

early 1980s at the offices of a business developer working for the City of Duluth.

At the time, Jack LaVoy had been involved with economic development for more than a decade, first as an economic development specialist with the Seaway Port Authority of Duluth (SPAD) and later as a business developer with the city. A native of Cloquet, LaVoy was a UMD graduate who served two terms in the Minnesota House of Representatives, from 1970 to 1974. "And it was there," LaVoy said, "that I began to become acquainted with Minnesota Power and some of the executives, particularly Jack McGrath, who was their head legal counsel at the time."

By the time he went to work for the business development staff at the city in 1979, LaVoy had been involved for several years in efforts to locate a paper mill in West Duluth. The effort to attract a new paper mill to Duluth can trace its origins back to 1976, when community leaders first learned that Blandin Paper Company was considering an expansion of its paper-making operations in Grand Rapids, Minnesota, by adding a new, high-speed paper machine to the company's existing mill.

LaVoy wrote years later, "the economy of northern Minnesota was relatively strong everywhere but in Duluth. To the north, sizeable investments were continuing to be made in increasing and upgrading taconite production capacity across the Iron Range. In the smaller communities dependent upon forest products, demand for paper and wood products remained strong, so strong in fact, that national business indicators demonstrated that investments in additional paper-making capacity for coated business papers could be justified nationwide. In response to those indicators, the leadership at Blandin Paper Company had begun making expansion plans."

Duluth, meanwhile, was experiencing the rapid erosion of its manufacturing base. Between 1972 and 1976, U.S. Steel closed its 60-year-old Duluth Works steel plant and neighboring Atlas Cement plant. More than 2,600 high-paying industrial jobs were lost as a result of the closures. An estimated 5,000 additional jobs were lost in supporting businesses. Almost overnight, the city had gone from being a strong, blue-collar, steel-making town to becoming the first spot of rust on what would soon be labeled the "Rust Belt."

The setbacks to the Twin Ports economy were part of a trend of plant closures that had gripped Duluth since the late 1950s when a number of Duluth-based mid-sized manufacturers such as Coolerator and Klearflax began to close.

LaVoy credited Robert Babich, the executive director of the Northeastern Minnesota Development Association (NEMDA), a private industry-driven economic development organization that had been heavily involved in the development of the area's taconite industry, with first suggesting locating a paper mill in Duluth. In 1976, Myles Reif, the CEO of Blandin Paper Company, agreed to assign a team to examine options for a Duluth site for a proposed Blandin expansion.

"It was at that time that I first became involved with the Duluth paper mill project as part of a task force set up by Mayor Robert Beaudin to work with the Blandin team," LaVoy said. "As various sites were assessed across the city, one in particular had what appeared to be an unbeatable advantage—a site in West Duluth adjacent to the mothballed M.L. Hibbard Steam Electric Station."

But enthusiasm for the proposed mill was quickly dampened by circumstances beyond the Duluthians' control. Reif's unexpected death in the midst of the process created an air of uncertainty over the plan's long-term potential. LaVoy began writing and calling paper company CEOs trying to drum up interest in the Duluth project. But by the spring of 1978, the project seemed dead.

The Engineering School Initiative

There the matter might have ultimately rested had not Jack Rowe taken on the task of securing an engineering school for his alma mater, the University of Minnesota Duluth. In the early 1980s Duluth was reeling from the loss of more than 5,000 jobs. The Duluth Air Force Base closing, Jeno Paulucci's decision to move his Chun King canned food production to southern Ohio and the shutdown of such longtime Twin Ports employers as Zalk Josephs, Clyde Iron, American Hoist & Derrick and National Iron had devastated the Twin Ports.

Economic development efforts were put in place to help right the job loss. Air base re-use efforts succeeded in bringing a minimum-security federal prison camp to Duluth, as well as adding another fighter wing to the Duluth Air Guard Base. The Duluth delegation to the Minnesota Legislature also was successful in securing legislative approval for the creation of a University of Minnesota-operated Natural Resources Research Institute (NRRI) at the former Duluth Air Force Base.

During the 1981 session, the Legislature also approved the creation of an engineering school at UMD. This was the key to the future of the Duluth paper mill project.

Local support for the proposed engineering school came from a group of regional engineers who joined together in establishing the Northeastern Minnesota Engineering Education Curriculum Council (NMEECC). NMEECC consisted of engineering executives from Minnesota Power, Hibbing Electronics, Potlatch Corporation and Reserve Mining Company.

Rowe had assigned Minnesota Power engineers to the engineering school project including Tom Ferguson, Dick Swenson and John Johnson, who served as managers for the Company, and perhaps most importantly, Bob Marchetti, the Company's senior vice president and one of Rowe's oldest friends.

Bob Marchetti grew up in the iron mining town of Ironwood in Michigan's Upper Peninsula. An engineering graduate of the then Michigan College of Mines in nearby Houghton, Marchetti joined Minnesota Power in 1950. The next year, Marchetti was working as an assistant engineer building the Syl Laskin Station when an even more junior engineer arrived at the construction site in Aurora. Marchetti and Jack Rowe would be best of friends for the next half-century. By the 1980s, Marchetti was senior vice president of power supply and engineering, ranking below only Rowe and Arend Sandbulte in the corporate chain of command.

Ferguson and Johnson were assigned to work with Jack LaVoy on the assignment at the capitol. Marchetti was a frequent visitor to St. Paul during the legislative session.

Senator Sam Solon stick-handled the engineering school project through the legislative process. It quickly gained vital support statewide and sufficient momentum to convince university officials not to oppose it. The bill was approved and signed by Governor Perpich with funding to establish two engineering programs at the Duluth campus, with the potential for future growth.

"We made some very valuable contacts in the Legislature that we leveraged for future efforts," Tom Ferguson said.

'Let's Do It'

The effort to establish an engineering school at UMD also paved the way for Marchetti and LaVoy to forge an even closer relationship. "Within a week after the Legislature adjourned," LaVoy noted, "I received a call from Bob Marchetti inviting me to lunch. He was pleased with our success and wondering if there were other opportunities where we could collaborate. He told me that now that we had the engineering school project under our belts, what should Minnesota Power and the city of Duluth start working together on next? And, I said to him, 'How about collaborating on trying to bring a new paper mill to Duluth?'"

At their luncheon meeting, LaVoy told Marchetti about the earlier efforts to attract Blandin Paper Company several years before, and said he had recently read an article in the *Wall Street Journal* and a similar one in *Business Week* that indicated that demand for high quality printing papers was once again exceeding supply. LaVoy added that the shortage was getting to a point where as many as 10 new paper machines could possibly be built in the United States over the next several years.

"So I said to Bob, 'Why don't we try to have one of those built in Duluth?'" LaVoy explained. "Bob's face lit up, and he responded with his usual enthusiasm, 'Let's do it!' And, at that moment, both of our lives began to change more than we could have imagined."

The pair's first focus was on Blandin Paper Company. The company was by then owned by Fletcher Challenge, a New Zealand-based forest products company that had purchased British Columbia Forest Products about a year before.

The city of Duluth had developed a modest public financial incentive package and some updated information showing how a paper mill might be developed in West Duluth near the M.L. Hibbard plant. LaVoy accompanied Duluth Mayor John Fedo, John LaForge, general manager of KDLH-TV, and Jack Rowe to Grand Rapids to make a presentation to Al Wallace, Blandin's new CEO. Wallace had not been involved with Blandin's earlier Duluth efforts, but he assured the group that he would read the report and give it full consideration.

The Lake Superior Paper Industries' mill on Duluth's bayfront quickly became America's leading source of supercalendered paper.

A month later, Fedo received a gracious rejection from Wallace. But in saying no, Wallace noted that "while Duluth has many tremendous advantages for developing a paper mill, for a variety of operational efficiencies, if we do add capacity, we will do so adjacent to our existing facilities in Grand Rapids."

Wallace's 'no thank you', but "Duluth has many tremendous advantages for a paper mill" was enough for LaVoy, Marchetti and Rowe. They proceeded with the idea that Duluth had the potential to be a paper mill town.

By early 1984, Minnesota Power had committed to economic development in the region, and Rowe and Marchetti encouraged LaVoy to continue pursuing the paper mill project. LaVoy promptly contacted Governor Rudy Perpich, who he had learned was having breakfast the next week with the president of St. Regis Paper Company. St. Regis operated a mill near Sartell, and LaVoy prevailed upon Perpich to give St. Regis the information he had developed for a Duluth mill.

Perpich gave the briefing material to the St. Regis executives, and about a month later, in March 1984, St. Regis sent a team of executives on

The Hibbard Plant on the bayfront in Duluth—built when Herbert Hoover was President of the United States—gained new life when it was refitted to furnish steam for LSPI.

a fact-finding mission to Duluth. St. Regis at the time was intent on adding a new coated paper machine, whether at a greenfield site such as Duluth or at one of the company's existing mills in New York or Maine. St. Regis was impressed with Duluth and asked if the city could do more to make the cost of steam more competitive. LaVoy called Marchetti and suggested setting up a municipally-owned steam district to help lower the cost of process steam.

Marchetti told LaVoy to ask Arend Sandbulte to look the concept over. LaVoy met with Sandbulte and explained that the city needed to create a publicly-owned steam district at the Hibbard plant similar to the one that had served the downtown Duluth area since the 1930s. "We could use tax-exempt financing to improve it and be able to produce steam at a cost-effective basis that would make the Duluth project work," LaVoy told Sandbulte. "And he said, 'Let me do some thinking and some calculating.' He did, and it was surprising how little time it took him to get back to me."

With the agreement for a steam district in hand, St. Regis was quickly won over to the Duluth site. In August 1984, senior executives of the paper company met at the Duluth Holiday Inn with Mayor Fedo and his staff and Minnesota Power personnel to finalize the proposal prior to presenting it to the St. Regis board later that month. The meeting had barely gotten under way when the phone in the room rang. It was the company's senior vice president calling to tell the St. Regis executives that international press lord Rupert Murdoch had just announced he was mounting a hostile takeover attempt of St. Regis. Once again, the Duluth paper mill project was dead in the water.

Finding Pentair

Neither LaVoy nor Minnesota Power gave up. They had a 92-acre site, competitive steam costs and a state-of-the-art wastewater treatment and recycling facility in the Western Lake Superior Sanitary District (WLSSD). LaVoy once again began calling potential expansion candidates. He quickly winnowed the list to two paper companies: Montreal-based Repap and Pentair of St. Paul.

Both companies agreed to visit Duluth to inspect the site. "When Pentair came up," LaVoy said, "it was obvious they were people similar in caliber, personality and character to the executive staff at Minnesota Power. And right away there was this sort of camaraderie or collegiality that was established between those two groups. Pentair decided to give us every effort to make our case, and we did. Pentair seemed to be a perfect fit."

Pentair CEO Murray Harpole liked the project and agreed it was more competitive than an expansion the company was contemplating at its mill in Niagara, Wisconsin. But Harpole told the city that Pentair did not have the financial clout to undertake such a project on its own. Pentair was interested in proceeding if Duluth could find it a joint venture partner.

For the next six months, LaVoy and Marchetti searched for a partner

Eugene Nugent, Pentair President; Tharlie Olson, Pentair VP; Tony Johnson, Pentair Executive VP; Bob Edwards, MP; Arend Sandbulte, MP; Jack Grunewald, Pentair VP and CFO; and Jack Rowe, MP, break ground for LSPI.

for Pentair. They talked to a Canadian company in Thunder Bay and had a preliminary discussion with a Norwegian paper company. In the spring of 1985, executives from Mitsubishi expressed interest. Mitsubishi agreed to meet with Pentair to discuss the concept, and LaVoy set up a meeting with Pentair and Minnesota Power at the paper company's Roseville, Minnesota, headquarters for mid-May 1985.

Since identifying Pentair as a potential owner of the Duluth paper mill, Marchetti and LaVoy often had discussed the possibility of Minnesota Power partnering with Pentair. LaVoy argued that a partnership would fit in nicely with the utility's diversification activities, which by then included telephone companies in Wisconsin and the Southwest and water plants in Florida. But each time LaVoy brought the matter up to Rowe and Sandbulte, they replied that Minnesota Power wasn't a paper company.

On May 19, 1985, Mayor Fedo and LaVoy from the city, a contingent from Mitsubishi, and Rowe, Sandbulte and Marchetti crowded into Pentair's Roseville boardroom. Harpole welcomed the group. He was joined by D. Eugene Nugent, Pentair's president, and Ron Kelly, the company's vice president of corporate development.

Kelly made Pentair's presentation. He told the group of about a dozen executives and city officials that Pentair intended to build a world-class mill in Duluth to make lightweight coated supercalendered paper, a grade commonly used in newspaper inserts that was in short supply in the United States. Kelly said if Mitsubishi decided to join them, the project would be completed on a fast-track basis.

It quickly became apparent that Mitsubishi wasn't ready to commit to such a high-speed schedule. "So as the formal presentations began to wind down and as the meeting was about to break up," LaVoy recalled, "Jack Rowe, Arend Sandbulte and Bob Marchetti asked for an opportunity to meet with Murray Harpole, D. Eugene Nugent and Ron Kelly. The rest of us were asked to wait so that we could wrap up the morning's events with lunch at a nearby country club."

The Minnesota Power and Pentair executives huddled for about a half-hour and then headed out to eat. At the lunch table, LaVoy sat next to Harpole, who informed him that it looked like Minnesota Power was going to partner with Pentair in the paper mill project. LaVoy earlier had told Marchetti that he was planning to leave the city business development office. Harpole asked if LaVoy would consider joining the partnership team. The next day, LaVoy was in Senator Sam Solon's office at the state capitol when Marchetti left a message.

"When I returned the call," LaVoy said, "he told me it appeared that the project would move forward and that Sandbulte had asked him to inquire whether I would be interested in continuing to work on the project after I left the city, only this time for the private sector."

LaVoy agreed, and in July 1985 he moved into an office at 30 West Superior Street. LaVoy and Pentair's Ron Kelly were the first full-time employees of the partnership, and, working with consultants and engineers, they rapidly completed a feasibility study for the new paper mill. There were a few hurdles to leap along the way. Part of the 92 acres to be redeveloped was an abandoned scrap metal yard with the potential for significant pollution. Governor Perpich stepped in and agreed to make the acreage part of an accelerated Superfund cleanup that would be remediated before construction got started.

Another stumbling block was Duluth entrepreneur Jeno Paulucci and his demands for compensation for a former Chun King building on the site. Although the matter was strenuously litigated, the city of Duluth used its condemnation powers to keep the project on schedule.

On October 23, 1985, Jack Rowe, Pentair's Eugene Nugent and Mayor John Fedo called a late afternoon press conference at the mayor's conference room on the fourth floor of Duluth's City Hall. The three men announced that Minnesota Power and Pentair were proceeding on the construction of a $350 million supercalendered paper mill adjacent to the Hibbard plant.

Mayor Fedo pointed out that the capital investment would be the largest dollar amount spent on a Duluth project since U.S. Steel built the steel plant in Morgan Park 70 years earlier. Fedo told reporters that the project would employ more than 1,600 construction workers during 1986 and 1987. When the mill did go into commercial operation in early 1988, it would employ 300 workers full time. An additional 300 northern Minnesotans would be employed in such ancillary occupations as wood procurement and transportation.

The partnership, which soon would become known as Lake Superior Paper Industries (LSPI), was the economic shot in the arm that Duluth had been searching for since U.S. Steel closed its Morgan Park steel works nearly a decade before. For Minnesota Power, LSPI was a clear signal that the Duluth Company was no longer the staid electric utility it had been for nearly 80 years.

"This venture will strengthen the economy of the Minnesota Power service area," Jack Rowe told the media at the October 23 press conference. "It will also help us diversify. It is consistent with our emphasis on economic development and diversification as a means of strengthening this community and this region."

CHAPTER 6 The Florida Land Boom

A century from now, when Minnesota Power is celebrating its bicentennial, historians will identify the fall of 1985 as the period when the economy of northern Minnesota started rebounding. Part of that rebound could be attributed to Minnesota Power's digression from its traditional electric utility model.

The economy of northern Minnesota changed when the taconite industry began its climb back to profitability. Although Butler Taconite's closing in 1984 sent shock waves across the Mesabi Range, the Nashwauk producer was perhaps a necessary victim of the shakeout in the iron and steel industry. The remaining taconite producers benefited from the reduced competition. The capacity shed in plant shutdowns meant that the survivors at least had the chance to sell their pellets profitably.

In the fall of 1985, Minntac and Hibtac, the two biggest producers on the Mesabi Range, signed amended take-or-pay Large Power contracts with Minnesota Power, signaling their intent to produce pellets into the 1990s. The amended contracts called for an 18-percent demand reduction, but they were significant for Minnesota Power because the taconite producers no longer were petitioning the MPUC for relief from their contracts.

The new contract extensions "benefit our area to keep the steel industry as competitive as possible," Arend Sandbulte told employees in November 1985. "Because of reduced demand for steel, the taconite companies had more power under contract than they could use. By getting contract extensions in exchange for reduced power under contract, we felt we could help relieve some of this area's uncertainty about the steel industry's future."

Two months earlier, Minnesota Power experimented with technological changes in the region's iron mining industry. In September, the Company unveiled its Mesabi Metal Project at a Hibbing press conference. Mesabi Metal was an innovative alternative iron technology that used taconite and coal to smelt direct reduced iron for making steel on the Mesabi Range. Mesabi Metal was probably 15 years ahead of its time, but it was an indication of Minnesota Power's willingness to make significant research and development investments in an attempt to make the local economy more competitive.

And the October 1985 announcement that Minnesota Power was joining St. Paul-based Pentair, Inc. in the construction of a $350 million paper mill on the bayfront in West Duluth set the capstone on the most ambitious economic development project in Duluth to that time.

Deltona

The news that Minnesota Power was diversifying into coated paper production overshadowed another event that took place in the fall of 1985 with equal, if not greater, impact on the Company's future. In September 1985, Topeka Group signed a letter of intent to invest more than $22 million in the preferred stock of Deltona Corp., a Florida-based land development and water utility operator.

Deltona was one of the creations of legendary Florida and Arizona land developer Del Webb and his partners, the Mackle Brothers. One of the most respected development firms in the Sunshine State, Deltona operated the Deltona Lakes community 26 miles northeast of Orlando, which had 31,000 homeowners. Deltona also developed Marco Island on the Gulf Coast south of Naples, and Spring Hill, a 30,000-resident community just north of Tampa-St. Petersburg. Deltona Corp. served nearly 60,000 water customers in the state. Its spokesperson was Bob Griese, the popular former quarterback for the National Football League's Miami Dolphins.

The firm fell on hard times in the 1970s when recession afflicted the Florida land development business. The Mackles also ran into a buzz saw of environmental opposition when they tried to develop Marco Island.

The development company thought it had attended to all the details when it started selling lots at Marco in the early 1970s. After some $20 million worth of lots on the tropical island had been sold, the U.S. Army Corps of Engineers refused to allow dredging of the property. Deltona lost nearly $60 million in the resulting imbroglio and lawsuits. By 1985, Deltona was ready to cut its losses and exit the Florida land business.

Topeka Group's Jack McDonald and Donnie Crandell had first become aware of Deltona's plight in the spring of 1985. Crandell and Phil Bergerson of Topeka Group had identified Deltona as a potential acquisition candidate shortly after Minnesota Power acquired Southern States Utilities as part of the Ray Dittmore transaction in 1984.

Topeka Group began negotiating with Deltona in the spring of 1985, and by that fall had agreed to purchase four million shares of a new issue of cumulative preferred stock in Deltona. The purchase price was set at $5.50 per share, and Topeka Group negotiated the option of purchasing an additional 545,000 shares of the stock within one year of closing the original transaction.

With four million shares, Topeka Group would control a 43-percent voting stake in the Deltona Corp. and had the right to name three members to the company's board of directors. Crandell told the Minnesota Power board that the investment in Deltona would return 10 percent in the near term, and that it allowed for the purchase of developable land or utility property at no significant premium over book value.

"It continues to position us as a stronger water utility in a high-growth region of the country," Crandell said, adding that Southern States Utilities was engaged in an ongoing effort to buy smaller water utilities in such Florida growth areas as Ocala and Gainesville. "We are continuing to negotiate with at least a dozen other small water and wastewater utilities in the central and northern areas of Florida."

Topeka Group closed its purchase of a 43-percent share of Deltona in early November 1985, but not before fending off a hostile takeover attempt of Deltona by a North Carolina toy manufacturer. Empire of Carolina, a Tar Heel toy and apparel firm, quietly purchased nearly 30 percent of Deltona's common stock in October 1985. Empire of Carolina then filed suit in federal district court in Miami to thwart the proposed Topeka Group investment.

Judge Stanley Marcus of Miami heard the case during the first week of November. After three days of testimony, Judge Marcus ruled that the competing claim was "without merit," and that Empire failed to prove its case. "Far from conspiring with the suitor at the expense of shareholders," Judge Marcus said, "Deltona played the only card it had."

Judge Marcus found that the Topeka Group offer was far superior to that of Empire of Carolina, ruling that "the evidence satisfies the court that the present financial condition of Deltona is bleak. The cash flow is negative. Deltona has been selling its assets, is delinquent in its debts and faces further deterioration."

With Deltona essentially in the fold, Topeka Group moved quickly to exercise control. McDonald and Roger Bowman, a Duluth realtor and former Minnesota Power board director, were appointed to the Deltona board. In the wake of the Empire of Carolina takeover attempt, the two new members from Duluth pledged to hire a national search firm that would select an independent slate of directors for the Deltona board.

Frank Mackle III, Deltona's president, expressed delight at the Topeka Group involvement. "This association accelerates our ability to solve old problems and focus on the development and sale of property," Mackle said at the closing. "Topeka is a strong business partner that we are confident will infuse new ideas and experience from different disciplines into our company."

The Deltona acquisition was a turning point in Minnesota Power's diversification initiative. With the purchase of Deltona, Topeka Group achieved critical mass in the Florida land business. For an initial investment of just over $30 million, Topeka Group became one of the major players in the Florida water and wastewater treatment business. Even more important, the investment positioned Topeka Group and Minnesota Power to become leaders in the Florida land development boom of the 1990s.

The Deltona investment included nine existing communities with 8,800 acres under master plans, 1,000 acres of unplatted property in close proximity to existing communities, and 1,450 acres of land outside the existing communities for future development. All told, Deltona had an inventory of 31,500 unsold, platted residential lots and commercial tracts.

In 1988, Topeka Group came close to selling its interest in Deltona to General Development Corp., another major Florida land development firm. The price negotiated for Topeka Group's investment in Deltona was $45 million, a 40-percent premium over the $32 million the firm had paid for Deltona's cumulative preferred stock just three years before.

The May announcement of General Development's interest was followed by negotiations during the summer of 1988 that led to an August announcement that Deltona and General Development would merge to form Florida's largest land development firm, with assets valued at $82 million. But in the final analysis, the two parties could not agree on future operating responsibilities and relationships. The merger agreement was shelved in early September 1988.

Building SSU

Meanwhile, McDonald's team at Topeka Group had been acquiring other water and wastewater utilities in Florida and the Southeast. In 1986, Minnesota Power's diversification subsidiary purchased Amelia Island Waterworks for $2.1 million. The water utility served 3,000 customers and

a world-renowned tennis complex in a resort community off Florida's East Coast, north of Jacksonville. Topeka Group spent $6.5 million to purchase the Venice Gardens Utility Corporation serving 12,000 customers in fast-growing Sarasota County, north of Fort Myers. The company also invested $6.5 million in preferred stock of Good/Gulfstream Holding Corporation for the option to buy the firm's Seminole Utility and its 5,500 customers in suburban Orlando.

SSU's wastewater treatment units served Floridians from one end of the peninsula to the other.

Topeka Group branched out in 1987 to make its first water and wastewater treatment acquisition outside of Florida when it purchased Heater Utilities, a water utility firm located in Cary, North Carolina.

The utility served more than 6,400 customers in the booming suburbs of Raleigh, North Carolina, and Columbia, South Carolina.

All of the late 1980s water and wastewater treatment acquisitions were operated under the umbrella of Southern States Utilities. To ensure that the growing customer load was handled with the same quality service that Minnesota Power electric customers had come to expect, Topeka Group embarked on a program of expansion for SSU. The water utility hired numerous maintenance and service personnel during the late 1980s. In 1986, SSU moved its headquarters to a new 14,400-square-foot building in Apopka, north of Orlando. The new facility included space for offices and centralized dispatch functions.

Sandy's Role

The Topeka Group's foray into diversification activities accelerated rapidly during the latter half of the 1980s, thanks to the work of McDonald, Crandell, Bergerson, and their team of analysts and development specialists. But the Group's ability to engineer complex deals half a continent away from Minnesota also was due to the strong support for diversification in the executive offices back in Duluth.

McDonald reported directly to Arend J. Sandbulte, the Company's president and chief operating officer. Sandy, as he was known to just about everybody at Minnesota Power, was a 20-year veteran of the Company and recently had been promoted to the number two spot at the utility. With his quick mind and background in electrical engineering and business administration, Sandbulte was admirably suited to head the Company's diversification efforts. Born in Sioux Center, Iowa, a Dutch farming community in the northeastern part of the state, Sandbulte was a 20th century Horatio Alger story.

"I was born and raised on a farm," Sandbulte said. "Until the eighth grade I went to a one-room country schoolhouse where all eight grades were in the same room and had the same teacher. My father bought an implement business in the town of Sioux Center in 1944. We moved into town in 1947, and I graduated from high school in 1951. I started dating my wife, Verna, in 1951, and we were married in 1953. I did not go to college right out of high school. I worked at the implement business. In 1954, I volunteered to go into the Army. I got inducted in March of 1954, spent some time in Aberdeen, Maryland, at the ordnance school, went over to France for a year in the service, and got out in December of 1955."

Sandbulte enrolled at Iowa State University in nearby Ames, and by attending school year-round, earned a B.S. degree in electrical engineering in just over three years. He had job offers from General Motors, General Electric and Northwestern Bell Telephone, and also was interviewed by Iowa Public Service in Sioux City and Northern States Power (NSP) in Minneapolis. Sandbulte couldn't make up his mind whether to take the job at NSP or at Iowa Public Service.

"My dad said to go to Sioux City because it's near home, and my heart said Minneapolis because I had a nirvana-type dream that we were going to live in Minnesota someday," Sandbulte explained. "So I took two letters to the post office. Both of them said, 'I'll take the job.' I said to Verna, 'I'm going to mail one.' She said, 'Do whatever you think.' So I mailed the one to NSP in Minneapolis and tore up the one to Iowa Public Service in Sioux City."

Sandbulte had been at NSP for five years when he was approached by Minnesota Power's Jennings Johnson, then

Sandbulte with Governor Rudy Perpich, 1989

the Company's assistant controller, in 1964 to head the Duluth utility's rate department. He was 30 years old and had just earned his M.B.A. at the University of Minnesota. Sandbulte and his family moved to Duluth in late 1964, and he began his meteoric rise at Minnesota Power. Ironically, the job he was first promised never materialized. The person he was supposed to replace in the rate department decided to stay with the Company, and Sandy found himself working as a financial analyst and assistant to Jennings Johnson. He eventually was named director of budgets and research, a newly established department.

In 1970, NSP approached Sandbulte about returning to the Minneapolis utility. Syl Laskin, then Minnesota Power's president and CEO, called Sandbulte into his office. He said Sandbulte had a good future at Minnesota Power, and he thought Sandy could be president of the Company someday. Laskin gave him a raise and named Sandbulte assistant vice president of corporate finance.

From then on, the promotions were almost constant. In 1974, Sandbulte became vice president of corporate planning. Two years later, he was named chief financial officer (CFO). In 1978, Laskin retired, Jack Rowe was named president, and the board of directors named Sandbulte senior vice president of finance and administration.

Two years later, Rowe announced that Sandy was the Company's new executive vice president. In 1983, he added the title of chief operating officer, and in 1984, Sandbulte was named president and chief operating officer when Rowe moved up to the position of chairman and CEO. In 1988, Sandbulte was named president and CEO. A year later, when Rowe retired, Sandy assumed the title of chairman, president and CEO.

From the beginning of the Company's diversification efforts in the early and mid-1980s, Arend Sandbulte was a prime mover behind Topeka Group's water and land projects in Florida and the Carolinas. Sandbulte also would be instrumental in strengthening the Company's core electric business as the industrial economy of northern Minnesota struggled to recover its equilibrium in the late 1980s.

CHAPTER 7 The Core Business

In 1986, approximately 225 investor-owned electric utilities served end-use customers in the United States. Most, like Minnesota Power, had their roots in the holding-company era and had been spun out as operating utilities serving states or regional areas when the holding companies were broken up during and after World War II.

Each year, the editors of *Electric Light & Power*, the trade magazine that followed the industry, selected one of those 225 companies as Electric Utility of the Year. In late October 1986, *Electric Light & Power* bestowed the prestigious award on Minnesota Power.

Minnesota Power's competition included such heavyweights as The Southern Companies, American Electric Power, Consolidated Edison and Pacific Power & Light. But as the magazine's editor, Robert Lincicome, explained, it was really no contest.

"The utility was selected for the strength of its performance in 1985 and to date in 1986," Lincicome said in a front page article in the magazine's November 1986 issue, "on behalf of its customers, shareholders and employees, with respect for the quality of life and the environment within its service territory."

Minnesota Power was the 16th utility in the nation selected for the award since the magazine first named an Electric Utility of the Year in 1969.

In an October 31 presentation to Chairman and CEO Jack Rowe and President Arend Sandbulte at Duluth's Kitchi Gammi Club, Lincicome explained that he long had been an amateur magician. "Magic doesn't happen when some rotund magician comes out on stage and pulls rabbits out of his billowing cape," Lincicome told the 150 guests. "Real magic takes place when some skinny magician comes out on stage in skintight leotards and pulls elephants out of his hat."

Pulling elephants out of a hat was less an optical illusion than it was a combination of management vision and hard work on the part of the entire Minnesota Power team. Rowe acknowledged the latter when he accepted the award on behalf of everybody at Minnesota Power. Rowe singled out employees for special praise. "They are the flesh and the blood and the brains and the heart of the power Company," Rowe said. "Blue collar, white collar, pink collar—in all their various jobs—they really are the Company."

Minnesota Power was recognized by its peers in the mid-1980s for the excellence of its utility operations.

And Holding the Line on Rates

Electric Light & Power's selection of Minnesota Power as Electric Utility of the Year was peer recognition of the Company's record of achievement during the difficult operating conditions in the first half of the 1980s. "When a utility's major industrial base goes into a steep slide and its service territory ceases to grow, it's tough for the utility to hold its own, much less improve its financial position and increase the scope of its activities and influence as a corporate citizen," Lincicome wrote in the magazine's cover story accompanying the award. "But 'improve' is exactly what Minnesota Power has done."

The magazine cited Minnesota Power for its 17-percent increase in net income in 1985. The $69 million in net income translated into earnings-per-share of $4.67, a 15-percent increase from 1984 and more than 80 percent ahead of 1980 earnings-per-share. "These substantial improvements," Lincicome wrote, "came despite only a one percent gain in revenues and an 11-percent decline in kilowatt-hour sales."

The financial performance was reflected in Wall Street's treatment of the Company's common stock, which reached record levels above $45 a share in early 1986. In fact, at the time Minnesota Power was being recognized, the Company's stock was undergoing a 2-for-1 stock split.

Electric Light & Power pointed out to readers that because of the utility's diversification and economic development strategies, Minnesota Power had transformed itself in less than five years. But, as befitting an award that recognized Minnesota Power as Utility of the Year, what the Duluth utility had accomplished in the core business of generating, transmitting and distributing electric power within its 26,000-square-mile service territory is what really attracted the magazine's attention.

"Not only has the Company prospered for shareholders," Lincicome explained, "but it has been able to hold the line on rates for customers." In fact, the Company's last rate increase had been five years before, in 1981, and Minnesota Power had told state regulators that it hoped to be able to realign rates in 1987 or 1988, without having to resort to further rate increases.

Bleaker and Bleaker

Northeastern Minnesota continued to absorb a series of economic body blows during the mid-1980s. The restructuring of America's steel industry that had seemed so drastic in 1980 and 1981 actually accelerated from 1984 to 1986.

By 1984, taconite mills were being shut down, padlocked and written off by their owners. When the Wheeling-Pittsburgh Steel Company became the first steelmaker in a generation to file for bankruptcy protection in April 1985, the reverberations quickly were felt on the Iron Range. Butler Taconite, one of the smaller producers and a Minnesota Power Large Power customer, closed its gates in Nashwauk permanently when its owners, Wheeling-Pittsburgh, Cleveland-based Hanna Mining Company and Inland Steel, were unable to sign contracts for the plant's pellets. The Butler closure alone cost 500 residents of the western end of the Mesabi Range their jobs.

The situation continued getting bleaker during the remainder of 1985 and 1986. In July 1986, LTV Steel, an integrated producer with roots in the earliest days of the industry, filed for bankruptcy protection. One of the victims of the LTV troubles was Reserve Mining Company, which supplied LTV's Cleveland and Indiana Harbor mills with pellets. Reserve, coming off a bruising, decade-long battle over its practice of dumping taconite tailings into Lake Superior, promptly ceased operations.

Although Reserve generated its own power at Silver Bay and was not a primary Minnesota Power customer, it did have significant back-up power agreements with the Duluth utility. Minnesota Power later won more than $20 million from Armco Steel Corporation, Reserve's parent, when a court ruled that the taconite producer had broken the power contract. Reserve also was a major employer in Lake and Cook counties northeast of Duluth. When partners Armco and Republic Steel Corporation dissolved Reserve in the spring of 1987, it was a sign of how far the fortunes of the taconite industry had sunk.

Another casualty of the LTV bankruptcy was Pickands-Mather & Co., managing agent for Erie Mining Co., in Hoyt Lakes and operator and 15-percent owner of Hibbing Taconite. The Cleveland-based firm had been involved in iron ore production in St. Louis County for almost a century. On the last day of 1986, Pickands-Mather was purchased by Cleveland-Cliffs Inc, its longtime competitor.

By early 1987, the U.S. steel industry had closed more than 30 million tons of capacity since 1977. A six-month lockout and work stoppage at USX Corporation only compounded the industry's woes. When the labor dispute was finally settled in February 1987, USX Chairman David Roderick announced that facilities employing more than 3,700 steelworkers wouldn't be restarted. A month later, the big Pittsburgh steelmaker extended its Minntac closure until summer, permanently laying off another 400 workers in the process.

More than 10,000 employees of the Iron Range taconite plants had been laid off or lost their jobs in just eight years. Thousands of Iron Rangers, many in their 20s and 30s, left Hibbing, Virginia, Chisholm and other Range communities for jobs elsewhere, often in the then-thriving oil and gas industry in Texas and Louisiana.

Renegotiating Contracts, Reducing Expenses

Minnesota Power's strategy for dealing with the continuing contraction of its taconite customers during the mid-1980s was twofold. The Company worked aggressively with its taconite customers to reduce their costs by renegotiating the take-or-pay power contracts. And Minnesota Power concentrated on reducing expenses so the utility could pass the resulting cost savings along to customers.

The strategy was realistic, given that industrial customers still comprised half of the utility's revenues. Even if the northern Minnesota economy diversified as fast as Minnesota Power's ambitious diversification efforts, taconite and pulp and paper processing would remain a major component of the regional economy. Minnesota Power knew it had to make its industrial customers as competitive as possible.

Minnesota Power negotiated with its Large Power customers throughout 1985. By year's end, the Company had signed extensions with U.S. Steel and Hibbing Taconite, the utility's two biggest customers at the time. Arend Sandbulte explained that from Minntac and Hibtac, "we got six-year and five-year-plus contract extensions, respectively, in exchange for reducing the contract demand for each by 18 percent."

The contract extensions offered to Hibtac, Minntac and Blandin Paper reduced Minnesota Power's 1986 revenue by $15 million. The revenue loss from the three customers was projected to drop to $3 million at the expiration of the contracts in 1991. The extensions also ensured that the Large Power consumers would remain Minnesota Power customers until at least the early 1990s.

"It benefits our area to keep the steel industry as competitive as possible," Sandbulte said. "By getting contract extensions in exchange for reduced power under contract, we felt we could help relieve some of this area's uncertainty about the steel industry's future."

By February 28, 1986, most of Minnesota Power's Large Power customers had agreed to some sort of extended contract in exchange for lower demand charges. But for Large Power customers attempting to escape their contracts with Minnesota Power, the Duluth utility was willing to draw a line in the sand.

"There was a big battle in 1987-1988 with National Steel," Sandbulte noted. "They tried to get out from under the contract. They said they were going bankrupt, that they had to go to bankruptcy court."

National Steel Pellet Company notified Minnesota Power in early 1987 that it intended to quit doing business with the utility when the contract expired at the end of 1988. National Intergroup of Pittsburgh and Nippon Kokkan of Japan, the joint owners of the Keewatin taconite producer, approached the Mid-Continent Area Power Pool (MAPP) and the Hibbing Public Utilities Commission about selling power to National Steel Pellet.

But in a precursor to the deregulation and open access battles that would roil the utility industry in the 1990s, Minnesota Power argued to the Minnesota Public Utility Commission (MPUC) that it was entitled to hefty compensation should Hibbing or MAPP wheel power over Company transmission lines to National Steel Pellet. The matter actually went to the Minnesota Legislature where it was bounced back to the MPUC on a tie vote. After encountering opposition from the MPUC, National Steel Pellet dropped the idea and ratified a contract extension with Minnesota Power in 1988.

The second part of Minnesota Power's core business strategy in the mid-1980s involved creating efficiencies that would allow the Company to reduce operating expenses wherever possible. Since fuel charges comprised a major share of electric power generation, Minnesota Power undertook a campaign to ensure low-cost power generated from coal for its customers for the remainder of the 20th century and beyond.

In the early 1980s, the Company was in litigation with the Burlington Northern Railway (BN) over proposed freight rate increases of almost 100 percent for hauling low-sulfur Powder River coal from Montana to Minnesota Power's Clay Boswell plant at Cohasset. When it appeared that Minnesota Power would be successful in pressing its case in court, the rail carrier approached the utility early in 1984 about renegotiating a long-term freight contract. Minnesota Power was more than willing to talk.

"Our strategic plans and goals have been to try to make arrangements and contracts for fuel supply for the life of our power plants," Sandbulte told the employee publication *Contact* in a lengthy interview. The Minnesota Power president immediately assigned Charles M. "Chuck" Reichert, vice president of administration, and Senior Attorney Phil Halverson to the sensitive negotiations. Ten months later, they emerged with a landmark contract.

Minnesota Power and BN in late 1984 signed a 15-year contract that included two five-year extensions exercisable by Minnesota Power. "So the

Unit train delivery of low-sulfur Montana coal benefited Minnesota Power ratepayers.

contract would extend through 2008 if we were to exercise the two five-year extensions," Sandbulte explained. "The contract takes care of us for 25 years, if we want to have it last that long, and 15 years in any event."

With the fuel supply and transportation issues locked up for a quarter-century, Minnesota Power continued to make aggressive moves to control costs in other arenas. The personnel reduction that the utility had put into place in 1980 after Clay Boswell Unit 4 came on line gradually reduced the number of full-time employees on the payroll without the utility resorting to the more drastic expedient of laying employees off. In 1985 alone, more than 50 Minnesota Power employees elected to opt for a Company special early retirement program. By 1986, Minnesota Power had reduced its work force by 200 employees, about 15 percent since beginning the effort in 1980.

Selling Capacity

Another strategy the Company implemented during the mid-1980s to reduce its core business exposure to adverse economic conditions in the steel industry involved sales of excess capacity to neighboring utilities. Following the 1980 completion of Unit 4 at Clay Boswell Station and the almost simultaneous collapse of the taconite industry, Minnesota Power had far more generating capacity than it needed. In 1985, the Company had slightly more than 1,500 megawatts of capacity, 82 percent generated from low-sulfur coal and lignite. System peak demand was just over 1,030 megawatts, leaving a reserve margin of 46 percent. Typical reserve margins

Computerization of power plant controls helped Minnesota Power run, maintain and dispatch its generating units at high levels of efficiency.

among other MAPP utilities at the time were in the 15 percent to 20 percent range.

In addition, Minnesota Power system peak demand wasn't likely to expand much before at least the mid-1990s. Jerry Ostroski, the Company's vice president of planning, estimated the peak system demand growth for Minnesota Power would only average about one percent a year through the late 1980s and early 1990s. He predicted that much of the Company's construction initiatives during that period would consist primarily of life extension efforts at existing generation and transmission facilities.

Other utilities in the Upper Midwest were capacity short, which presented Minnesota Power opportunities for selling some of its excess capacity. In late 1985 and early 1986, Montana-Dakota Utilities (MDU) retired old steam generating units at various sites in its North Dakota, Montana and South Dakota service territory. The Bismarck, North Dakota, utility, which lost 29 megawatts because of the capacity retirements, was a partner with Minnesota Power in Coyote, a North Dakota lignite station built during the 1970s.

When MDU purchased a 12-megawatt share of the Big Stone lignite plant in South Dakota in the spring of 1985, Minnesota Power quickly inquired if the Bismarck utility had any interest in buying it out of Coyote. MDU was receptive to the idea, and between 1986 and 1988, it acquired Minnesota Power's five-percent ownership share of Coyote, totaling 21 megawatts.

An even bigger capacity sale was announced in early 1986 when Minnesota Power and Minneapolis-based Northern States Power (NSP) reported that they were close to signing an agreement for NSP to purchase a 207-megawatt share of Clay Boswell Unit 4 and a 100-megawatt purchase of the Duluth utility's Square Butte entitlement. The proposed agreement was slated to go into effect between 1989 and 1991. However, NSP exited the deal before it could be consummated.

With the reduction in capacity ownership in the mid-1980s, Minnesota Power had cut its reserve margin nearly in half. Just five years later, however, the economy in northeastern Minnesota was turning around, and it was beginning to look as if Minnesota Power might need the capacity for the 1990s.

CHAPTER 8 | On the Rebound

Transformation of Duluth's Canal Park into a tourist destination got underway during the mid-1980s.

When it finally came, the economic rebound was incremental—but pronounced, nevertheless. Northeastern Minnesota began a sharp recovery in the late 1980s, and by the early 1990s, transportation, taconite and timber— the three 'Ts' of the local economy—were exhibiting signs of surprising strength. A fourth 'T'—tourism—was providing much-needed jobs, especially in the economically distressed Duluth-Superior area.

Minnesota Power's vote of confidence in the regional economy, primarily through the investment in the new Lake Superior Paper Industries (LSPI) mill in West Duluth and other economic development initiatives in northeastern Minnesota, was just one aspect of the region's recovery. Between 1980 and 1988, the administration of President Ronald Reagan had conquered inflation and cut taxes, giving business the incentive to invest in core manufacturing industries such as steel and pulp and paper.

At the other end of the political spectrum, the administration of Governor Rudy Perpich, a native of the Mesabi Iron Range, had taken a special interest in restoring the health of the state's often neglected Arrowhead Region. Perpich's interest in the economic well-being of his home region often was enough to convince investors that northeastern Minnesota was on the way back. And Governor Perpich frequently had legislative support for his economic development initiatives. Many of the key committee seats in the Minnesota House and Senate during the 1980s were held by Iron Range and Duluth politicians such as Willard Munger, Doug Johnson, Joe Begich, Mike Jaros and Sam Solon.

An Energy Crisis in Remission

One final factor played into the revival of the late 1980s and early 1990s. By 1990, the energy crisis that had plagued the American economy since the oil embargo shocks of 1973 and 1979 was finally in remission.

Natural gas supplies, in particular, rebounded sharply after the 1979-1980 heating season, putting the industry into a surplus position that it did not work out of until mid-decade. A deregulation mandate laid down by 1978 federal legislation transformed the industry during the 1980s, creating a model by 1990 for other segments of the nation's utility industry.

Suddenly in the early 1980s, natural gas pipelines and local distribution companies had more gas and fewer markets. The so-called natural gas "bubble" had been born. That was good news for Mesabi Range taconite producers, who used immense amounts of natural gas in processing raw iron ore into pellets. Gas prices fell sharply by mid-decade and gas reserves at the time were growing at an average rate of 7 percent a year, helping steel company executives in their decisions to reopen taconite mills.

Cutting Costs

By the late 1980s, Minnesota's Mesabi Range was in the midst of an economic recovery. Nobody seriously believed the industry would ever again achieve the 60 million-ton production level of 1979, but a leaner, more efficient industry held the promise of producing in the neighborhood of 40 to 45 million tons of pellets each year.

The revival of the area's taconite industry in 1989 and 1990 was a confirmation of trends Minnesota Power had already identified. As far back as 1986, Minnesota Power executives had consulted nationally known steel industry executives to gauge the potential recovery. The Rev. William T. Hogan, a Fordham University professor of industrial economics with several books to his credit and one of the most respected steel analysts in North America, was in Duluth in early October 1986 to brief Minnesota Power executives and planners on the industry's future course.

"Iron ore will continue to be a significant item" in the manufacture of steel, the relatively bullish Hogan told the Minnesota Power team. Hogan

High-voltage transmission towers surrounding a Mesabi Range taconite mill illustrate the symbiotic relationship between electric power and contemporary iron mining.

predicted that the industry would remain concentrated in a narrow band along the lower Great Lakes between Chicago and Cleveland. Such a concentration, Hogan said, meant that "the Mesabi Range will continue to provide pellets to the basic oxygen process mills."

Less than a week later, Peter Marcus briefed the Minnesota Power group on his outlook for iron and steel. Marcus, chief iron and steel analyst for PaineWebber, was perhaps more pessimistic than Hogan about short-term prospects. But as publisher of *World Steel Dynamics*, a steel reporting service with clients around the world, Marcus had a global perspective on the industry that Minnesota Power wanted to hear.

Marcus stressed that domestic finished steel pricing had gotten so low because integrated producers had to deal with foreign and mini-mill competition. Captive iron ore producers in Minnesota and Michigan simply had to continue shaving costs if they wanted to remain the suppliers of choice for the integrated, blast furnace segment of the industry.

Marcus noted that taconite producers were in the process of reducing the cost of pellets from the posted lower lakes price of $47 a ton to a spot price of $30 to $35 a ton. The most competitive producers, including Minntac and Hibtac, were then producing pellets delivered to South Chicago at about $38 a ton, with projections for further cost reductions, Marcus said.

In 1986, Minnesota Power was cooperating with taconite customers to help them slash costs. The take-or-pay contract extensions and reduction in demand charges had decreased the cost of electric power to taconite producers by more than 1 cent per kilowatt-hour in just three years. Average kWh charges for Minnesota taconite producers dropped from 5.91 cents to 4.88 cents between 1983 and 1986. Charges would drop another cent, from 4.88 cents to 3.84 cents, between 1986 and 1989.

Even more dramatically, the spread between electricity costs for Minnesota producers and their counterparts in Michigan significantly narrowed during the 1980s. In 1983, Minnesota taconite producers paid almost one cent per kWh more than Michigan producers. By the end of the decade, that margin had been narrowed to less than a tenth of a cent.

A vehicle parked inside a bucket puts into perspective the size of the equipment used in taconite mining.

Lower energy costs, coupled with productivity gains, led to a steep drop in the cost of ore production by 1989. The productivity gains during the period were as impressive as the drop in energy costs. In 1981, the average mine in Minnesota produced just under two tons of pellets for each employee hour worked. Six years later, the production per employee hour worked had nearly doubled, to 3.8 tons of pellets.

Using such procedures as computerized pit dispatching, increased flexibility in job classification, changes in work assignment, reduction in plant maintenance and an increased pace in work, Minnesota's mines increased productivity. New technology, including 240-ton trucks and shovels with 38-yard dippers, replaced earlier models of mine equipment.

Fluxed pellets, which came on the market in the mid-1980s, were more efficient than their predecessors. Fluxing pellets involved baking the ore and clay mixture at the taconite kilns with limestone to produce a more easily reduced pellet for the blast furnace. Minnesota's taconite producers by the end of the decade could meet or beat the threat of foreign competition, primarily Brazilian ore landed at Chicago.

The rebirth of Minnesota's taconite industry was a cumulative affair, but if observers needed to identify a date for the actual turnaround, 1987-1988 was as good as any. "Everybody's tremendously optimistic," Al Harmon, then Minnesota Power's director of marketing, said early in 1988 of the Duluth utility's taconite customers. "They're on a roll."

Dr. Peter Kakela, a professor of resource development at Michigan State University and one of the world's experts on iron ore production, told Minnesota Power executives at year-end 1987 that he thought the iron ore industry had bottomed out in 1985. "The U.S. steel industry is now competitive with world steel," Kakela said, "and that's going to play back reasonably directly to iron ore."

The productivity gains meant that the vast majority of the miners laid off during the 1980s would never return to work. By the end of the decade, only 5,500 people worked in the region's taconite industry, down from more than 16,000 in 1979. But by achieving significant savings in the cost of making pellets, the taconite industry participated in the upturn when the American economy rebounded at the end of the 1980s. As a result, Minnesota's taconite companies ended the decade with production of 40 million tons of pellets, the best performance since 1980.

Reopening Reserve

Cleveland-Cliffs, the owner and manager of iron ore properties in Minnesota, Michigan and Canada, took part in the event that signaled the final resurgence of the Iron Range. In 1989, Cliffs made a bid for the assets of Reserve Mining Company. Reserve had closed several years earlier when its steel mill managing partners couldn't find solvent customers for the Silver Bay plant's pellets.

The closure had devastated Silver Bay and surrounding communities on the North Shore of Lake Superior. Silver Bay's population dropped 40 percent to fewer than 1,900 people as unemployed miners headed south to the Twin Cities or Texas for job opportunities. Reserve had been one of 19 North American pellet plants closed during the 1990s.

But when Cleveland-Cliffs and Cyprus Minerals engaged in a bidding war to buy the Reserve assets, they ensured that the taconite facility would be one of a few to revive. Although Cliffs outbid Denver-based Cyprus Minerals by $1 million, a bankruptcy judge approved the Cyprus bid for the plant, which was valued at $680 million.

Cyprus spent $30 million to upgrade the Silver Bay facility and its pit near Babbitt, and launched Reserve as Northshore Mining Company in 1990. Northshore began operations as a non-union plant and sharply scaled back to 4.5 million tons of pellet production per year, but its reopening heralded a rebirth of an industry many had thought dead. Minnesota Power quickly began negotiating with Cyprus for an electric service contract at Northshore. Four years later, in 1994, Cyprus sold its ownership in the

Silver Bay taconite facility to Cleveland-Cliffs, opening the way for the Cleveland-based iron ore producer to become Minnesota's most important taconite player.

Opportunities in Pulp and Paper

While the taconite industry slowly clawed its way back to profitability in the late 1980s, the pulp and paper industry, Minnesota Power's other Large Power class of customers, was enjoying a strong expansion as the decade wound down. Much of the paper produced in northern Minnesota mills was lightweight coated paper. Paper making enjoyed a rapid expansion in the late 1980s as Americans switched to desktop personal computers and printers.

Minnesota Power's fast-track construction of Lake Superior Paper Industries' mill in West Duluth brought a significant new load onto the utility's system. Launched in 1987, the new mill rapidly captured 20 percent of North America's market for supercalendered paper and by 1989 shipped more than 215,000 tons.

A wave of expansions at existing pulp and paper mills began in 1988 when Blandin Paper Company, the original candidate to build LSPI, announced it was planning to spend $400 million to modernize the company's Grand Rapids pulp mill and to install a new paper machine. The Blandin expansion was slated to be completed by 1990 and would

The forests of the upper Great Lakes provide a sustainable fiber resource for the pulp and paper industry.

increase production by nearly 80 percent. When in full operation, the Blandin expansion was projected to double its electric power needs.

Next to announce a major plant expansion was Idaho-based Potlatch Corp. With a mill at Cloquet, Potlatch long had been the mainstay of the Carlton County economy. The expansion of the Cloquet mill included the addition of a new paper machine, an off-machine coater, a supercalender,

winder, roll storage area and computerized roll-handling system. When finished in 1989, the $500 million investment increased the Cloquet mill's electric power needs from nine megawatts to 15 megawatts.

Later in 1989, Boise Cascade Corp. announced the addition of a paper machine at its mill in International Falls. The Boise expansion, estimated at $535 million, was at the time the largest private

Expansion of northeastern Minnesota's pulp and paper industry led the region's economic recovery during the late 1980s. Blandin Paper Company pictured.

industrial investment in Minnesota's history.

In the expansions at Potlatch and Blandin, Minnesota Power had acted as a traditional electric utility, investing capital to build new substation and transmission facilities to handle the increased load. But Minnesota Power took more of a partnership role in the Boise expansion. In 1989, Minnesota Power signed a memorandum of understanding with Boise in which it agreed to build a cogeneration plant for providing steam to the new machine at the International Falls mill.

"A cogeneration project is well-suited to the International Falls mill and will provide another major employment opportunity for Minnesota construction workers," Al Harmon explained to local media. Harmon noted that Minnesota Power engineering staff was designing the 45-megawatt facility. What would become Rainy River Energy started operation of the first of two boilers in late 1990. The second boiler began providing steam to Boise Cascade in early 1991.

Canadian pulp and paper manufacturer MacMillan Bloedel Ltd. completed the late 1980s expansion of Minnesota's forest products economy when it invested $75 million to build a new board mill at Deerwood to serve the homebuilding market in the Upper Midwest.

Capacity Questions

The resulting upturn in the region's economy flowed directly back to Minnesota Power's bottom line. Already by 1988, the Duluth utility was setting record peaks. Usage peaked at almost 1,200 megawatts in December, exceeding a peak set in 1981. By 1990, sales of 10.2 million Megawatt-hours (MWh) established an all-time record.

The proposed 1986 capacity sale to Northern States Power had been withdrawn a little more than a year after it had been negotiated.

The complex transaction had been approved by the Minnesota Public Utility Commission. The Federal Energy Regulatory Commission (FERC) had agreed to the transaction in 1988, but had deferred a decision on whether the purchase price would be reflected in NSP's wholesale rates or its retail rates. Minnesota Power and NSP appealed the FERC ruling. Minnesota Power even offered to indemnify NSP for that portion of the gain FERC might ultimately refuse to allocate to the Minneapolis utility's rate base.

NSP sued in the summer of 1988, asking a Minnesota court to void the agreement to purchase the Boswell capacity. Early in 1989, Minnesota Power counter-sued, arguing that NSP had breached the contract. Minnesota Power eventually prevailed.

In 1989, Minnesota Power still wanted to shed excess capacity from Boswell Unit 4. But by that time, the utility envisioned selling a smaller percentage of the Cohasset plant. In August 1989, Minnesota Power sold a 20 percent share, about 100 megawatts, of Boswell Unit 4. Wisconsin Public Power Inc. (WPPI), the joint action agency serving municipal power utilities in the Badger state, agreed to buy the capacity effective October 1990. The sale was subject to Board approval by both parties, regulatory approval of the sale and arrangements to transmit the power across the NSP transmission grid.

"Joint ownership of this power plant will help us bring our generating capacity in line with what we expect our customers will require in the 1990s," President and CEO Arend Sandbulte told analysts and the media. "In addition, this sale will help Minnesota Power remain one of the lowest priced providers of electricity in the U.S., which is good news for our customers."

Sandbulte's optimism was well-placed. The partnership with WPPI has worked extremely well for both parties for more than 15 years.

Refining Diversification

The recovery of the regional economy in the late 1980s and the boost to Minnesota Power earnings due to a surging core electric power business was accompanied by a redirection of the utility's diversification efforts. As Minnesota Power came closer to the 1992 deadline for deriving 25 percent of its earnings from diversified investments, the utility made some strategic decisions on how it would reach that goal.

It had become apparent in 1988 and 1989 that Minnesota Power would be better able to grow the Florida water and wastewater treatment subsidiaries than to buy additional rural telephone systems.

Shortly after acquiring UTI from Ray Dittmore, Minnesota Power had assigned Donnie Crandell to investigate growing the diversified business. "We started engaging consultants to go and introduce us to small independent telephone companies," Crandell said. "But with the AT&T breakup, which was going on at the same time, there was a buying frenzy in the industry. People were paying exorbitant prices. We spent three years going up blind alleys. We never added another purchase in the telephone business."

On a parallel track, Crandell had also begun looking at the possibility of growing the Company's water business. In 1984 and 1985, he was a regular visitor to the Orlando and Miami areas, conferring with Southern States Utilities' Tom Kravitz and Charles Sweatt about growing the water and wastewater business in Florida and the Southeast.

"We decided there was a huge market potential," Crandell said. "I thought there was a real business there."

Crandell moved to the Orlando area in 1986 to take charge of water and wastewater acquisitions. After considering a 1988 offer from a respected Florida residential real estate developer to buy a controlling interest in the Company's subsidiary, Deltona Corp., Topeka Group terminated the discussions. The next year, Topeka Group more than doubled SSU's water customer base when it acquired Deltona's water utility subsidiaries. Topeka Group exercised an option it had held since 1985, when it provided Deltona a substantial cash infusion.

Divesting UTI

Minnesota Power would begin the 1990s with more than 135,000 Florida water customers, thanks to Topeka Group's exercise of the Deltona option. The Company would start the decade with no telephone customers.

On March 3, 1989, Sandbulte announced that Topeka Group had signed a letter of intent with Century Telephone Enterprises, Inc., for the sale of the outstanding capital stock of UTI, Topeka Group's telecommunications subsidiary. Century agreed to pay $90 million for UTI's 47,000 telephone access lines in Wisconsin and four other states. Five years before, Topeka Group had paid $20 million for the stock in UTI, which also included the Florida water properties of Southern States Utilities.

The decision to divest UTI had been difficult, but one which was necessary if Minnesota Power was to expand its water and wastewater treatment properties. Century Telephone, a Monroe, Louisiana-based telecommunications firm with operations in 12 states, was willing to pay a premium for UTI because the Minnesota Power subsidiary's 37,000 Wisconsin customers complemented the 45,000 customers Century already served in the Badger state.

"UTI was a good investment," Sandbulte told shareholders in the spring of 1990. "But to achieve our diversification goals we needed to expand that business by buying other telephone companies. We tried for five years to add to Universal, but couldn't buy a system at what we considered a reasonable price."

Acquiring BNI

Minnesota Power ended the 1980s with one final diversification initiative, this time a vertical integration closer to home. Its involvement with Square Butte Electric Cooperative during the previous decade had introduced Minnesota Power to the lignite coal suppliers of western North Dakota. A low-sulfur coal, lignite met increasingly stringent federal and state air quality standards. Lignite could be burned at power plants in relatively unpopulated North Dakota and sent by transmission wires east to load centers in Minnesota and Wisconsin.

In August 1988, Minnesota Power announced a merger agreement with Baukol-Noonan, Inc., of Minot, North Dakota. Under terms of the

A dragline operator at BNI Coal scoops up another load of North Dakota lignite.

A BNI dragline as large as a house mines a seam of lignite coal for the Milton R. Young Generating Station near Center, North Dakota.

$28 million agreement, Baukol-Noonan became a wholly owned subsidiary of Minnesota Power when the deal closed at year-end 1988. With 150 employees and yearly production of 3.5 million tons of lignite for Square Butte and Minnkota Power Cooperative's Milton R. Young Generating Station, Baukol-Noonan was one of the more active lignite mining firms in western North Dakota.

In announcing the merger, Sandbulte said that "this transaction is another step in our goal of diversifying the Company's activities into familiar areas." He also noted that Minnesota Power and Baukol-Noonan had enjoyed a successful working relationship for many years.

In mid-July, Chuck Reichert, Minnesota Power's vice president for administration, moved to the new corporate offices of Baukol-Noonan in Bismarck as the coal company's new president. Reichert, a native of Mandan and a graduate of the University of North Dakota, would guide the fortunes and growth of the renamed BNI Coal into the 21st century.

For Minnesota Power, the 1980s had been a period of upheaval and uncertainty. Electric utility deregulation would make the 1990s no less uncertain.

CHAPTER 9 Dealing with Deregulation

Electric utility deregulation first came to Minnesota Power's attention in dramatic fashion in early 1987. As the new year unfolded, the Company faced some key choices. Taconite customers were still showing signs of business malaise, with a corresponding stagnation in the utility's kilowatt-hour sales and revenues.

One taconite customer was actively fighting Minnesota Power to void its electric power contract. National Steel Pellet Company was adopting a novel strategy to play the contract negotiations out in the media. The Keewatin taconite producer was negotiating with Basin Electric Power Cooperative in North Dakota to purchase excess capacity from a Wyoming coal-fired power station. Under the plan, Basin would wheel the power across North Dakota and northern Minnesota to the Hibbing municipal utility, which in turn would sell the electricity to National Steel Pellet.

National Steel Pellet put on a full-court press in the media and the Minnesota Legislature, arguing that Minnesota Power's high electric rates were driving it out of business and endangering more than 600 jobs on the Mesabi Iron Range. Minnesota Power countered that National Steel Pellet was one of the taconite producers in the mid-1970s that had asked the Duluth utility to build new base load generation to serve the fast-growing industry.

Minnesota Power contended that it would be forced to lay off hundreds of employees if National Steel Pellet were successful in its attempt to breach the contract. Finally, Minnesota Power executives told reporters and legislators, the Company was in the process of slashing costs and offering extended contracts to taconite customers. Those contracts would reduce electric rates more than a penny a kilowatt-hour, some 20 percent less than the rates offered in the original contracts.

Jack Rowe, then in his last year as chairman and chief executive officer, warned about the potential loss of Minnesota Power jobs. "It's one of the most critical challenges to face us since I've been here," Rowe told Company managers at the utility's annual management conference in early February 1987. "Minnesota Power's future as a separate and viable Company is threatened."

Wearing sweatshirts that proclaimed "stop the monopoly" and "sink the Rowe boat," National Steel Pellet employees and retirees picketed Minnesota Power's Duluth headquarters and at the Minnesota Legislature during the winter of 1987.

The Minnesota Legislature wisely handed the dispute to the proper authorities, in this case the Minnesota Public Utility Commission (MPUC). But Minnesota Power couldn't be sure how the MPUC would treat the issue of Large Power contract extensions and open access to the transmission grid.

"The reaction at the MPUC was always an uncertainty," said Al Harmon.

The MPUC wasn't ready to unilaterally overturn electric utility deregulation in the state, and the National Steel Pellet matter was allowed to quietly die. But the proposal to wheel power for resale through a municipal utility customer created the impetus internally for a closer study of deregulation.

Early in 1987, Minnesota Power appointed an internal task force to study the potential impact that deregulation would have on the Company and Minnesota. Members of the Competition/Deregulation Investigation (CDI) Task Force studied every aspect of the problem, including the energy supply situation in the Upper Midwest, utility restructuring efforts elsewhere in the nation and steps Minnesota Power could initiate to become more competitive.

Steve Sherner, director of system operations, was named chairman of the CDI steering committee. He was joined by Kevin Robb, Gerry Van Tassel, Tom Lyden, Karen Evens, Chuck Pleski, Dave Gartzke, Al Harmon and Jim Roberts.

The State of Deregulation

The CDI team quickly discovered that utility deregulation was more than just talk. About the time the task force was chartered, Martha Hesse, the incoming chair of the Federal Energy Regulatory Commission (FERC), was warning utility executives that competition, deregulation and open access to transmission grids definitely was on the horizon.

Jim Roberts, for one, agreed with Hesse. The Company's manager of governmental affairs, Roberts had been on the front line of the bruising fight with National Steel Pellet in the 1987 session of the legislature. Roberts, a Texas native who began with Minnesota Power in 1974 as a janitor at the Syl Laskin plant and worked his way up through the ranks, spearheaded the Company's lobbying efforts during the tumultuous 1987 legislative session.

"I think it's likely we'll be operating in a modified regulatory environment in a few years," Roberts told CDI team members in the summer of 1987. Regulatory reform and least-cost planning would be two concepts that Minnesota Power would become much more familiar with in the years ahead, Roberts told the CDI team.

Roberts pointed out to the CDI Task Force that Hesse's warning represented a political philosophy that was changing the ground rules of nearly a century of utility operation. Both Presidents Jimmy Carter, a Democrat elected in 1976, and Ronald Reagan, a Republican elected in 1980, were strong deregulation advocates. Carter and Reagan believed that loosening federal regulation would encourage competition and innovation in American industry. Both presidents argued that cutting the red tape of regulation would eliminate monopolistic practices and lead to lower prices for consumers.

Reagan's administration oversaw the substantial deregulation of industries that had been tightly regulated since the 1930s, including trucking, airlines, banks, securities firms and railroads. Gas and electric utilities soon followed.

Congress passed the Public Utilities Regulatory Practices Act (PURPA) in 1978, and the U.S. Supreme Court ruled the legislation constitutional in 1982. PURPA's avowed aim was the deregulation of the natural gas industry, but the legislation also contained provisions that would nudge the electric utility industry toward deregulation. The PURPA legislation provided for the creation of non-utility generators (NUGs) and independent power producers (IPPs), both of which could build power plants and sell wholesale electricity on the open market to utilities or industrial facilities.

Federal policymakers quickly came to the conclusion that building more non-utility power plants would not necessarily foster deregulation or competition in the wholesale electric utility industry. IPPs, NUGs and their typically industrial customers complained that utilities were charging high tariffs on their high-voltage transmission systems to discourage competition. Open access to transmission systems, essentially what National Steel Pellet had asked the legislature to approve, was the next step in the nation's move to utility deregulation.

The Politics of Wheeling

The Minnesota Power CDI team was five years ahead of much of the rest of the electric utility industry in its attempts to assess the potential impacts of deregulation. In 1992, Congress passed the National Energy Policy Act. The legislation authorized electric utilities to begin investigating the feasibility of transmission access, the physical and legal ability of a power plant to use the transmission grid for the purpose of sending electricity to an end-use consumer.

Also known as wheeling, transmission access was critical to opening up the industry to deregulation and competition. Without open access, electric power consumers would be captive to the electric utility that generated electricity in their particular geographic area.

High-voltage transmission grids became the topic of state utility deregulation legislation in the 1990s.

The states followed the federal lead on utility deregulation, and in 1993, Nevada passed a limited transmission access law. The Michigan Public Service Commission approved a five-year retail wheeling experiment in the spring of 1994. Soon after, California passed the nation's most sweeping utility deregulation legislation.

But California's disastrous experience with utility deregulation was a cautionary tale for the nation's public utility commissions. In 1996, California's legislature enacted a law that effectively would implement retail electric competition in the state beginning in early 1998. Computer software problems delayed startup until March 31, 1998.

After that date, customers of the state's three major investor-owned utilities—Pacific Gas & Electric, Southern California Edison and San Diego Gas & Electric—had the choice of staying with their existing utility or selecting a new energy provider. Customers who elected to stay with their original utility were rewarded with an immediate 10-percent rate decrease that couldn't be lifted until 2002.

The enabling legislation also created the California Power Exchange, a non-profit public benefit corporation charged with operating a "spot market" for buying and selling electricity. The state's three investor-owned utilities were required to sell all the power they generated to the power exchange. Municipal utilities, independent power producers and utilities outside California had the option to sell to the exchange or sell directly to a customer.

The California experiment went horribly awry in 2000 when unscrupulous energy traders gamed the system and manipulated electricity prices to unheard-of levels.

Nobody understood the ramifications of full-scale utility deregulation when Minnesota Power's CDI Task Force submitted to management its recommendations for dealing with competition and regulatory reform. Although at the time they seemed to be timid and conservative, the Task Force's suggestions to enhance Minnesota Power's commitment to customer service and productivity improvements were the right approach to conditions that appeared more threatening than they actually were. In hindsight, the CDI team's proposals set in motion a cultural transformation at Minnesota Power.

"Evolutionary, Not Revolutionary"

In one of his first statements as Minnesota Power's new president and chief executive officer, Arend Sandbulte noted in late 1987 that the pace of change for Minnesota Power would likely be "evolutionary, not revolutionary."

The evolutionary changes were making themselves evident by the late 1980s and early 1990s. Rainy River Energy, the subsidiary that Minnesota Power created in 1988 to generate process steam for Boise Cascade's expanded paper-making operation in International Falls, was completing the installation of a 180-ton boiler at the Boise Cascade plant, the largest boiler ever shipped in one piece. The utility's cogeneration team was already investigating the potential for signing up additional customers for Rainy River Energy's services.

Another Minnesota Power subsidiary that was representative of the change in the utility industry was formed in late 1990 to pursue business opportunities in energy efficiency. Synertec's stated goal was to sell efficiency, resource and solid waste management, and pollution prevention services to commercial, industrial and governmental customers. As part of Minnesota Power's strategy to help customers become more competitive in their national and global markets, Synertec was aligned with the Company's strategic focus on customer service.

Named to head the Synertec initiative was Jerry Ostroski, the Company's vice president of planning. Ostroski recalled that he was asked "to see if we could make investments in the area to again grow the assets of the region profitably with some sort of an environmental hint to them. And out of that effort we looked at many, many things."

Members of the Synertec team, including Eric Norberg, Tony Pekovitch, Lynn Roginski, Phil Bergerson and Dick Swenson, studied a number of potential investment opportunities.

"We looked at the manufacture of lightweight aggregate products from paper mill sludges," Ostroski said. "We looked at the feasibility of building a plant to do that and then shipping the material out of the region.

We looked at making silicon metal, primarily because there was electricity available in this region. When you look at a piece of silicon metal, it is basically frozen electricity. And it takes a tremendous quantity of electric energy to make the silicon that's used in caulks and the material that's in computer silicon chips. We just couldn't put together a reasonable package there."

Construction crews worked around the clock to build Superior Recycled Fiber Industries (SRFI) in Duluth in 1992.

The Synertec strategy was to concentrate on one project and do it well. In late 1991, Synertec brought a project to the Minnesota Power board of directors that it recommended the utility consider backing. Superior Recycled Fiber Industries (SRFI), a partnership between a Synertec subsidiary and Lake Superior Paper Industries (LSPI), was a clear response to the nation's growing concern with using recycled, post-consumer waste for pulp and paper production. At the time, the new administration of President Bill Clinton was encouraging American industry to recycle.

Construction of the $76 million SRFI facility on a site adjacent to LSPI got under way early in 1992. The new plant was slated to employ 30 people when it went into commercial operation late in 1993. Synertec projected that the new facility would recycle 120,000 tons of office waste paper in its first full year of operation.

Before ground was broken for the new plant, SRFI had negotiated contracts for 70 percent of its pulp production during the first five years of operation. Most of the contracts were with area pulp and paper producers. Ostroski and his staff estimated that the new plant would consume nearly six percent of the office waste collected in the United States.

Good Customer Service

The early 1990s were a transition period for Minnesota Power and many U.S. electric utilities. Some neighboring utilities, such as NSP, became convinced that the best way to combat the threat of deregulation was to get bigger through mergers with other utilities and overseas power project partners. Other area utilities, such as OtterTail Power, pursued a diversification strategy that saw the utility go as far afield as the ownership of motels and minor league baseball teams.

Minnesota Power remained committed to its focus on customer service. As a result, the Company's marketing efforts took on added importance after 1990.

Minnesota Power, like most utilities in the Upper Midwest, had been built on marketing initiatives during the period from the 1920s to the 1950s. The Company's sales department had introduced a generation of northern Minnesota families to the luxury of electric appliances, and in the process had spearheaded Minnesota Power growth for more than 30 years.

Like most other utilities in the region, Minnesota Power had de-emphasized its sales efforts during the growth of the 1960s and 1970s. Public utilities commissions, including the MPUC, used the oil embargoes and energy crises of the 1970s to order electric utilities to halt appliance sales. But when the bottom dropped out of

A Company representative conducts a free energy audit at a customer's home.

the iron and steel industry in the early 1980s, Minnesota Power once again began to look at how to sell electric power to customers.

The reconstituted marketing department was organized under Al Harmon in 1986. Perhaps the Company's best known residential marketing effort at the time was The Electric Outlet, a retail shop on the ground floor of Lake Superior Plaza. Duluth native Lori Collard completed her economics degree at the University of Minnesota Duluth in 1979 and soon after went to work in Minnesota Power's rate department. Collard joined the marketing department when it formed in 1986 and would eventually be named the department's head. At the time, The Electric Outlet had been in business about three years.

"The original intent of the first Electric Outlet was to provide high-efficiency appliances to a market where they were not readily available," Collard explained. "And then, as those appliances became more readily available, the direction that The Electric Outlet went was to get more into electronics, more into the higher-end, new-to-market electronics. We were probably one of the first retail outlets up here to have VCRs on our shelves."

The Electric Outlet later expanded to a second store at Duluth's Miller Hill Mall and was restructured in the mid-1990s as The Electric Odyssey. Collard noted that the retail store's major contribution to Minnesota Power was to give the Duluth utility a brand identity for its marketing initiatives.

While Minnesota Power was involved with The Electric Outlet for more than a decade, the retail facility wasn't the utility's only marketing effort. "We were marketing high-efficiency water heaters," Collard said, "and then started the Dual Fuel program after 1985. It was becoming much more affordable with construction retrofits to put in baseboard heating. Homeowners had a lot more control, room by room, because of Dual Fuel. They would get a much cheaper rate. So we really were primarily pushing water heating and space heating on the residential side."

On the commercial side, one of the marketing department's areas of emphasis was lighting. "We became experts in commercial lighting, learned all about lighting, including how to actually design lighting systems and getting people to light up their businesses," Collard said. That was one area of major emphasis. Another area of emphasis was commercial cooking. We spent a lot of time with institutions, restaurants, getting them to put in electric cooking appliances."

Minnesota Power's first foray into electric power residential sales in more than a generation was The Electric Outlet.

At the same time, Minnesota Power engineers and energy technicians accelerated their work with customers on using electric power efficiently. Conservation efforts, first mandated by the MPUC in the wake of the 1973 and 1979 energy crises, continued throughout the mid-1980s. By 1990, Minnesota Power was spending $760,000 a year in its residential Energy Conservation Improvement Program. The Duluth utility spent more than half of that total in conjunction with 16 area weatherization agencies and community energy councils. Most of the programs were designed to assist low- and moderate-income homeowners and renters in improving the energy efficiency of their dwellings.

The Minnesota Legislature upped the energy conservation stakes the next year when it passed the 1991 Omnibus Energy Bill. Included in the legislation was a provision that mandated the state's utilities spend at least 1.5 percent of their gross electric revenues on conservation improvement measures.

Under the new legislation, Minnesota Power ramped up its expenditures for energy conservation to more than $3 million a year. Much of the increased spending was earmarked to help commercial and industrial customers improve lighting, as well as the efficiency of motors and manufacturing processes. John Gustafson, an engineer in the marketing department, explained that just over $1 million was available in 1991 for grants to assist the Company's Large Power customers.

"We are trying to get Large Power customers to see electricity as part of the solution and not part of the problem," Gustafson said. "If we get more financially sound customers, the end result will be to make Minnesota Power a more stable, financially sound Company."

The 1991 Omnibus Energy Bill was a clear indication that Minnesota state government was a long way from loosening regulatory control of the state's utilities.

CHAPTER 10 Paying Environmental Dividends

I
n early 1993, Arend Sandbulte concluded his letter to
shareholders in the Minnesota Power annual report
by pledging the utility's wholehearted support of
environmental quality.

Minnesota Power's stewardship of riparian lands in the St. Louis River basin includes management of the ecosystem for recreation purposes.

"One of our most cherished values is environmental
stewardship," Sandbulte said. "That's why we have chosen
'Environmental Dividends' as the theme for this year's
annual report. Respect for the environment is not a
burden we carry, but a value that inspires, lightens our load. And, we have
found, it is also good business."

To stress the importance of environmental leadership to his readers,
Sandbulte enclosed a full-page copy of the Company's environmental
ethics statement.

"Recognizing that all human activities affect the natural environment,"
the statement began, "the people of Minnesota Power are sensitive to
the environmental effects of our conduct as individuals and collectively
as a Company. We will be leaders in environmental stewardship. And,
consistent with public policy, we will:

- Meet or surpass all environmental compliance criteria.
- Seek and adopt safeguards to prevent injury to the environment,
  and be prepared to respond quickly should an accident occur.
- Promote land, air, water and energy conservation by encouraging
  customers and employees to use our products and services efficiently.

- Solicit public and regulatory agency views about environmental concerns and Company activities."

In addition, the Company's environmental ethics statement promised that the Company and its employees would seek ways to reduce adverse environmental impacts of utility activities, prevent waste by stressing efficiency and recycling, enhance the environment while carrying out Company responsibilities, and demonstrate conservation of land, air, water and energy.

Deeply Rooted

The promise to pay environmental dividends and treat its surroundings in an ethical manner was a philosophy deeply rooted in Minnesota Power's past. M.L. Hibbard, Clay Boswell and Jack Rowe, Sandbulte's predecessors as Minnesota Power chief executives, were all enthusiastic anglers and hunters, fiercely protective of the lakes, streams and forests of the Northland.

When Governor Harold LeVander singled out Minnesota Power in 1970 for "its many environmental contributions to the state of Minnesota, particularly in pollution abatement," Company president Syl Laskin accepted the award. Laskin, in turn, pointed to Hibbard as the inspiration for the Company's environmental consciousness. Hibbard, Laskin said, "implanted in all of us who worked with him the attitude that we are stewards, not owners of the environment… that we are doing things that affect the environment, and we have to be concerned about that."

When LeVander recognized Minnesota Power's environmental efforts, the federal government was passing landmark clean air and clean water legislation. The early 1970s were a time of ferment in American society. Dissatisfaction with the nation's role in the Vietnam War led to protests by young people on college campuses across the United States. The demonstrations continued as the war wound down, changing focus to the state of American environmental quality.

Between 1971 and 1973, Congress passed and President Richard M. Nixon signed landmark environmental legislation designed to improve the nation's air and water quality. The 1973 establishment of the federal Environmental Protection Agency created a mechanism to enforce the tough new environmental laws. Minnesota, anticipating the national trend, had created the Minnesota Pollution Control Agency (MPCA) in 1967.

Early federal and state environmental legislation targeted the coal burned by the nation's utilities as a prime contributor to the degradation of air quality standards. At the time of the passage of the Clean Air Act, Minnesota Power already was a pioneer in the utilization of low-sulfur coal that was fully compliant with the 1970 congressional legislation.

In 1968, Minnesota Power was already utilizing low-sulfur compliance coal from Peabody Coal Company's Big Sky Mine in the Powder River Basin of Montana. That year, Minnesota Power signed a three-way agreement with Peabody and the Great Northern and Northern Pacific

Railways to haul coal 850 miles from the Montana mine to Minnesota Power's Clay Boswell Station at Cohasset. The two railroads, both predecessors of the Burlington Northern Railway, agreed to haul the coal from Montana to Minnesota in 105-car unit trains, delivering 12,500 tons of the low-sulfur coal.

Sophisticated pollution control equipment called "scrubbers" were installed at Boswell Unit 4 in 1980.

"I think Minnesota Power was the first one in Minnesota to receive unit train shipments," Jim Marshall, then the Company's fuel administrator, said in a 1983 interview. "I think you can say that Minnesota Power... opened up western coal to the Midwestern states."

To fully comply with the 1970 clean air legislation, Minnesota Power budgeted more than $9 million for pollution abatement equipment at three power plants it was in the process of building or upgrading. Half of the money was allocated to wet scrubbers, a cooling tower, improved fly ash and processed waste disposal at the Company's Boswell Unit 3, then under construction.

A Formal Environmental Function

Much of the early environmental activity at Minnesota Power was handled as part of the Company's construction and fuel initiatives. In 1974, Minnesota Power established a formal environmental department. Eldon Kilpatrick, who had been handling the federal and state air quality permitting for Units 3 and 4 at Clay Boswell Station, was named the department's first director. The original employees of the department were Dennis Van Tassel, Steve Berguson, Cliff Olson and Bob Hoffman. The next year, Dave Hoffman, a Vietnam veteran with a doctorate in biology from the University of Minnesota, joined the department.

"When I moved to Duluth in 1975, Pat (Kilpatrick) and his staff were doing all of the Boswell 4 permit work," Hoffman recalled. "Later in the 1970s and into 1980 or so, we started working on the Floodwood-Fine Lakes permits. That was going to be a huge new generating facility. I think it was planned for 800 megawatts, and the state people wanted a complex capable of siting 2,400 megawatts so they didn't have to continue going through the same siting process. We also looked at the environmental ramifications of adding another unit at Square Butte."

Hoffman, who had written his doctoral dissertation on air quality monitoring around power plants, immediately was the Company's expert on Prevention of Significant Deterioration (PSD) standards. Two weeks after going to work for Minnesota Power, he found himself aboard the Company aircraft, bound for Washington, D.C., with Syl Laskin, the Company's president and CEO.

"They wanted me to do a presentation for the Minnesota congressional delegation," Hoffman recalled. "They said there would be three or four of us on the program, and I figured it would be mostly congressional aides. Instead, when we got to the hearing room, mine was the only presentation. And there sitting in the front row was Walter Mondale. Next, in walks Hubert Humphrey. Remember, this is just a couple of weeks after I started."

Hoffman's presentation noted that overly strict PSD standards had the potential of blocking further development of the state's taconite and forest products industries. Minnesota Power strived to balance protection of natural resources with the economic growth of northeastern Minnesota.

The Politics of Power Lines

Management of the land surrounding Minnesota Power's hydro system and the right-of-way surrounding northern Minnesota transmission lines contributed its share to the Company's environmental initiatives. Dave Jeronimus was a Duluthian who earned his degree in natural resources management at the University of Minnesota and then served six years in the United States Navy, part of that time flying attack aircraft off carriers in Southeast Asia. Jeronimus, who returned to the Twin Ports in 1973, was working on his master's degree in ecology when Minnesota Power hired him to write environmental reports for the DC transmission line the utility was building from North Dakota to near Duluth.

"It was somewhat of an informal function," Jeronimus recalled of the early environmental efforts. "When I was hired, I was hired as an assistant engineer. I worked for the manager of engineering, George Ferrario, and

Jerry Roettger was the director of the department. Bob Marchetti was the vice president."

Jeronimus noted that Minnesota Power exceeded what was required when siting transmission lines. "We did not at that point have to comply with the Minnesota transmission line siting act," he said. "But we thought it would be a good move from the standpoint of meeting and getting along with the people living along the power line corridor. So we went out and did public hearings, which were not yet required. Other utilities did not do that, and they ended up in a big controversy that lasted for quite a number of years before they got their transmission lines sited."

Jeronimus remembered being impressed by the top-down commitment to environmental quality that Minnesota Power exhibited from the start. From Syl Laskin to Jack Rowe to Arend Sandbulte, Ed Russell, Dave Gartzke and Don Shippar, Jeronimus never worked for a CEO who didn't take seriously the Company's need to protect the environment.

"Boswell 4 was by far the cleanest unit in the state at the time," Jeronimus said. "It was designed to carry you for the next 10 years, because we all knew the environmental emission standards would be ratcheted up over the years. It's much easier to put in something cleaner ahead of time than it is to try to go back in and re-engineer something at a later date at a higher expense."

In fact, Minnesota Power had designed the environmental controls for Boswell Unit 3 to exceed all existing standards. Almost 35 percent of the $400 million cost of Boswell Unit 4 consisted of pollution control system investments. The initial environmental controls at the unit removed 99 percent of particulate matter and nearly three-quarters of the sulfur dioxide released during the process of burning the low-sulfur Montana coal. The cooling towers installed as part of the Unit 4 environmental controls removed 2.5 million BTUs of thermal heat per hour from the plant's recirculating water.

Air emission standards at the Laskin Energy Center were similar to those in effect at Clay Boswell Station. When the M.L. Hibbard Station in Duluth was retrofitted to provide process steam for LSPI in the late 1980s, it, too, met or exceeded all federal and state air quality standards.

"Even back in the days of Syl Laskin and Jack Rowe, the basic feeling was that we needed to produce cost-effective power, reliable power, power that's environmentally compliant," Jeronimus said. "That was what we were directed to do, and that's what everyone did."

Stewards of the Land

Completion of Boswell Unit 4 and the high-voltage transmission grid that crossed northern Minnesota didn't end the need for a full-fledged environmental department. During the 1980s, Jeronimus and his colleagues

Boulder Lake Management Area, established in 1992, consists of 12,000 acres of land and water just north of Duluth. It is cooperatively managed by Minnesota Power, the Department of Natural Resources and the St. Louis County Land Department.

worked with the inventory of thousands of acres of land that Minnesota Power owned. Most of the land was acquired early in the 20th century when the utility was creating a hydroelectric power system on the rivers of the Northland.

Minnesota Power provided stewardship for the land, much of it north of Duluth and surrounding the Island, Boulder and Whiteface reservoirs, through a number of projects. Those included a timber management program, wildlife enhancement projects, raptor breeding efforts, fish propagation in the lakes of the reservoir system and aquaculture research.

In the 1970s, Minnesota Power signed an agreement with the Minnesota Department of Natural Resources (DNR) for resource management of the reservoir system. Minnesota Power agreed to lease

Fishing for walleye is a way of life in the North Country.

land to the state for boat-launching ramps, picnic areas, parking spaces, campgrounds and other improvements to the state for a nominal cost. The Company also promised to protect the remaining shoreline.

Minnesota DNR Commissioner Bob Herbst lauded the Company "for spearheading this effort not only to make its lands and reservoirs available to the public, but also its efforts to develop appropriate recreational facilities and protective measures for these valuable resources." Herbst noted at the 1972 dedication ceremony for the reservoir recreational facilities that "the taxpayer comes out the winner, since the lands are his to use judiciously without the costly acquisition often necessary."

Balancing Obligations

When Minnesota Power's environmental department was formally established in 1974, the Company realized it had to balance its obligation to provide electric power to customers while taking into account the cost of environmental regulations. Minnesota Power was ever mindful of meeting the public's expectations as a good corporate environmental steward. But the utility also understood the necessity of providing a sound return on investment for shareholders.

The key to achieving balance was cooperation. "Just throwing money at environmental problems won't fix them," a Company environmental services technician said in 1992. "Government, industry, environmental groups and the public all have the mutual goals of a cleaner environment. What we need to do is work cooperatively to achieve them."

In the spirit of cooperation, Minnesota Power environmental services employees served in dozens of state and local agencies, industry groups, trade associations and community organizations. Company employees worked with such groups as the Lake Superior Partnership, the Electric Power Research Institute's (EPRI) Whole Tree Energy Systems demonstration and the Adopt-A-Highway project.

Minnesota Power environmental affairs staff worked closely with a variety of public and private groups who hoped to better the environment. Minnesota Power's environmental services department employees lent their expertise to a broad range of outside interests.

In the 1980s and early 1990s, Minnesota Power's environmental services department expanded as the utility encountered a host of environmental issues including acid rain, electromagnetic fields (EMF), global warming and hydro re-licensing. Environmental issues had become so complex and politically charged that the Company's lobbyists asked for the expertise of an environmental staffer when pursuing Minnesota Power's interests in St. Paul and Washington, D.C.

Jeronimus, who retired as vice president of environmental services at Minnesota Power in 2004, recalled that the size of the department grew rapidly during the 1980s. "As we built Boswell 4, the environmental requirements mushroomed significantly. I think at one point we must have had upwards of 35 people in the department. That would have been between 1980 and 1985. We had to do all kinds of studies, and we could hire the people to do the studies cheaper than getting a consultant to do them."

Environmental Dividends

The environmental team that protected the St. Louis River by training for spill prevention and hazardous material control at the utility's Thomson Hydro Station was highlighted in the Company's 1992 annual report. The annual report noted that in 1992 Clay Boswell Station emitted sulfur dioxide at only 25 percent of the rate allowed by the federal government and the state of Minnesota. The plant's compliance with federal and state air emission standards saved Minnesota Power about $350,000 in air quality penalty fees in 1992.

Minnesota Power's environmental dividends carried over to diversified operations in Florida and North Dakota. Southern States Utilities (SSU), the Company's Florida water subsidiary, worked with 4-H clubs to promote water conservation at a time when much of the southern half of Florida was enduring a decade-long drought. The Apopka utility pointed out that outdoor irrigation could account for as much as half of the water consumed by residential customers.

SSU's Environmental Landscape Management Project involved planting drought-tolerant plants native to the region. SSU's innovative programs predated Florida's move in the late 1980s to mandate that utilities offer water conservation programs as a condition of water use permits. At Marco Island, water utility engineers installed an innovative reverse osmosis desalinization facility to conserve precious fresh water in the aquifer underlying Southwest Florida.

The Florida water operations "were very minimally staffed," Jeronimus said. "We spent a lot of time working with them and helped SSU develop its environmental audit program and environmental management system. At one point, they had 130 water and wastewater discharge permits; we had maybe a dozen. So they had a lot of ground to cover, and they did an excellent job of staying on top of everything."

In western North Dakota, Minnesota Power environmental engineers worked with staff at BNI Coal to restore the 175 to 200 acres of North Dakota prairie mined each year. BNI's draglines stripped the prairie overburden and mined the acreage to provide the lignite coal burned at the nearby Milton R. Young generating station. Since 1970, BNI had reclaimed almost 2,000 acres, planting shelterbelts, creating wetlands and transforming mined land into cropland and native grassland. Land that once was mined again supported mule deer, antelope, sharp-tail grouse and songbirds.

A farmer harvests small grains from reclaimed mine land in the shadow of the Milton R. Young Generating Station.

Reducing waste in the landfills of the Northland long had been a goal of Minnesota Power's environmental services department. In the early 1990s, the Company unveiled an innovative partnership between LSPI and the adjacent M.L. Hibbard plant. The paper mill provided the power plant with wood waste that was mixed with water and low-sulfur coal to make steam for the paper mill. Later, the power plant was fueled entirely with wood waste from LSPI and other regional sources. The Minnesota Pollution Control Agency recognized LSPI in 1991 for finding a productive use for 63,000 tons of bark, chips and wood waste that otherwise would have gone to a Duluth landfill. At Boswell Station, Minnesota Power landfilled the ash produced by the Hibbing municipal utility's steam station in a licensed, qualified disposal facility.

State agencies were not the only Minnesotans to recognize Minnesota Power for its environmental efforts. In a 1992 telephone customer survey, 500 people were asked how Minnesota Power was treating the environment. Two-thirds of the respondents said their utility was doing an excellent or good job at protecting the environment.

21st Century Environmental Initiatives

Protecting the environment is a cumulative endeavor. Regulations change. Air emission standards that were deemed suitable in 1992 are unacceptable in 2006. Alternative energy sources that were judged uneconomical or unworkable a decade ago hold the promise of baseload sources of power supply in the future.

Minnesota Power has never rested on its environmental laurels. When the state of Minnesota promulgated rules to increase wind energy generation for Minnesota electric consumers, MP immediately began seeking partners to help it in securing wind power assets. In the summer of 2005, the Company signed a long-term agreement to purchase 50 megawatts of wind energy from a new wind generation project to be built in south central North Dakota by a subsidiary of FPL Energy.

Renewable energy derived from wind turbines drove much of the electric utility industry's capacity growth in the 21st century.

The wind farm, located just north of the Milton R. Young Station near Center, was planned to be the state's largest when it broke ground in the spring of 2006. Once completed, the Oliver County Wind Energy Center will be capable of generating enough electricity to power more than 16,000 homes. Construction of the 22 wind turbines was expected to be complete in late 2006.

"Minnesota Power is here today to break ground at this site and declare our commitment to this project as part of our strategy of building a more diversified generation portfolio," Company Chairman, President and CEO Donald J. Shippar said in remarks at the April 19, 2006 groundbreaking. "A lot of thought and teamwork has gone into the project so far, and we are excited to get the real work started today."

MP continued to pursue plans to locate a second new wind farm on Minnesota's Mesabi Iron Range. Partners for the proposed project included FPL Energy and Iron Range Resources.

Minnesota has long prided itself on the quality of the air that state residents breathe, and MP has been keenly attuned to meeting and exceeding air emission standards at its fossil fuel power plants for an equally long time. In the fall of 2005, Minnesota Power unveiled its Arrowhead Regional Emission Abatement (AREA) plan designed to sharply reduce sulfur dioxide and nitrogen oxide emissions at the Taconite Harbor Energy Center in Schroeder and the Laskin Energy Center in Hoyt Lakes.

State regulators quickly approved the $60 million AREA plan, and Minnesota Power began to install new emissions control equipment at the two facilities in the fall of 2006. "Minnesota Power has an excellent environmental record," ALLETE President, Chairman and CEO Don Shippar said, "and we take stewardship of the land, water and air very seriously. Building on this historic commitment, we believe that control and abatement technology applicable to these plants has matured to the point where further significant air emission reductions can be attained through AREA in a relatively cost-effective manner."

An even more ambitious air emission abatement project followed hard on the heels of the AREA improvements. Early in 2006, Minnesota Power announced plans to reduce mercury emissions by up to 90 percent and to cut nitrogen oxide and sulfur dioxide emissions at the Company's Boswell 3 generating unit in Cohasset.

The second largest electric generating unit operated by Minnesota Power, the 350-megawatt Boswell 3 already operates at 70 percent below existing air emission requirements. Using Best Available Control Technology, Minnesota Power will spend $200 million to eliminate nearly all particulate matter emissions at Boswell 3 by installing a baghouse, flue gas desulfurization scrubber, low nitrogen oxide burners and selective catalytic reduction units.

The Minnesota Pollution Control Agency was expected to approve permits for the project in 2006, with all work slated to be completed by year-end 2009.

"The Boswell Unit 3 upgrade builds on our track record of stewardship in a region that is home to the Boundary Waters Canoe Area Wilderness, Voyageurs National Park and the Apostle Islands National Lakeshore," Shippar said in announcing the initiative. "Minnesota Power has a long history of successfully achieving and exceeding environmental requirements while providing competitive, reliable electric service to the region."

CHAPTER 11 New Directions

Minnesota Power entered the 1990s a vastly different company than just 10 years before. What had been a classic electric utility in 1980 was now a diversified energy services provider with interests in a number of states and lines of business.

Minnesota taconite and forest products customers still purchased the lion's share of electric power generated by the Duluth utility, but the Company quietly had built one of the largest water utilities in fast-growing Florida. LSPI, the Company's paper mill subsidiary, was one of the nation's most productive supercalendered paper producers. Minnesota Power had bought and sold UTI telecommunications when it couldn't grow the rural telephone system. The utility's BNI Coal subsidiary was a well-respected mining firm in the lignite fields of North Dakota.

The transformation in the Company's business changed the way that Minnesota Power's employees approached their assignments. Traditional electric utilities had modeled themselves after industry giants such as General Electric. They were process-oriented, tended to be bureaucratic because of well-defined chains of command, and relied on top-down decision making to get things done.

In 20 years of ALLETE leadership, Florida Water evolved into the largest privately held water and wastewater treatment company in the Sunshine State.

Arend Sandbulte was among the first at Minnesota Power to realize that employees would have to embrace a new corporate culture if the utility was to be successful as a diversified energy services provider. Sandbulte understood that Minnesota Power employees in the years ahead would face unprecedented challenges on two fronts, in the electric utility sector of the business and in the diversification activities. Sandbulte instinctively knew that competition was coming to Minnesota Power and other electric utilities, and competition already was a way of life in some of the subsidiaries the Duluth utility had acquired, including LSPI and BNI Coal.

To survive and prosper in the coming world of competition, Minnesota Power employees would have to be quick to identify opportunities and take advantage of them. They would have to be people-oriented and purpose driven—but flexible. In short, they would have to be far more entrepreneurial than Minnesota Power employees of the past.

In a 1989 interview with *Wall Street Transcript*, a respected investment publication, Sandbulte explained that the Company was embarking on a five-year project designed to change Minnesota Power's corporate culture. He hastened to add that the project wasn't a criticism of current employees, but a recognition that the employee of the future simply had to react to perform his or her job differently.

"We are pretty good now," Sandbulte told the interviewer, "but we could be better in terms of team orientation, participation, commitment and feeling of ownership by the employees. Much of the decision making now is taking place at a level higher than it needs to be."

Minnesota Power had discussed cultural change for much of the 1980s. Quality circles, a method for management and labor to address ways to cooperate in pursuit of goals, had been a staple in the customer operations and power supply departments since at least mid-decade. Progress had been made in such tangential areas as paperwork reduction. But Sandbulte wanted a maximum effort to affect cultural change at Minnesota Power.

During the next five years, Minnesota Power achieved change through Organizational Development.

O.D.

Organizational Development—O.D., as it soon became known at Minnesota Power—rolled out in the spring of 1989. Sandbulte announced the formation of an O.D. team that would be located off-site in downtown Duluth. Team members included a broad cross section of employees, including Warren Candy, Claudia Scott Welty, Bill Carlson, Marsha Fleissner, Tom Foucault, John Heino, Edie Houck, Steve Leino, Peter Olbin, Chuck Pleski, Al Hodnik and Bruce Overson.

Team leader was Warren Candy, a 39-year-old Australian who had come to the Northland with his wife, a Minnesota native, and found work at Clay Boswell Station. Growing up in Melbourne, Candy had worked in factories while attending the city's Swinburne College of Technology three nights a week. He identified with working people, telling colleagues about the days he ran a lathe in a Melbourne pump factory, "working when it's 110 degrees outside, up to your knees in metal casings, dirt, dust and sweat."

Sandbulte and Candy knew that cultural change wouldn't be simple to effect. "There was somewhat of a protectionist environment here," Sandbulte said. "Some people felt like once they got out of college, they could go to work here and be here for the next 40 years. I was saying at that time that if you're willing to be relocated, reeducated, if you're willing to do that, then you will have a job with us."

Sandbulte admitted his philosophy on entitlement employment gave some of the members of the O.D. team "heartburn," but it was an indication of how serious the normally soft-spoken CEO was about the necessity for change. He noted that O.D. simply was "trying to get people to step up and do what was necessary without necessarily being told what to do. I think that this was kind of a top-down culture, and O.D. was more of a get the job done, check for resources, get the resources you need."

Candy stressed that O.D. wasn't going to be "quick or easy. People don't resist change. They resist being changed." If O.D. initially caused confusion, Candy explained, it was because "if O.D. were a program, there would be more structure. But O.D. is not a program." Candy pointed out that O.D. team members knew that organizational development potentially was threatening, but he said that more and more employees would get involved in the effort in 1990 and 1991.

At the 1990 management meeting, Sandbulte laid to rest some of the employees' fears. "We don't want people to worry about their jobs and have them looking over their shoulders all the time," he said.

Candy credited Sandbulte with making O.D. work. "I think about Sandy in terms of the leadership that he provided to this organization during the time when obviously the taconite industry was imploding on itself back in the late 1970s and early 1980s," Candy said. "Then, how he came up with a plan to change the fundamental nature of this organization from a very small Company in northern Minnesota to what we've become today, and how he shepherded that through."

In 1990, Candy moved back to Boswell as plant manager. He was promoted to vice president of generation operations in the early 1990s, and was promoted to senior vice president of utility operations early in the 21st century, with responsibility for generation, transmission, distribution, Superior Water, Light & Power and BNI Coal.

Changing the Culture

Candy's replacement as team leader of the O.D. effort was Claudia Scott Welty. An Iowa native who grew up in Mankato, Welty moved to Duluth and completed her degree in communicative disorders at UMD. She worked for several years writing civil service exams for the City of Duluth before being hired in Minnesota Power's human resources department by Ollie Houx in 1979. For the next 10 years, she primarily worked with employee benefits and pay systems.

Welty's appointment to the O.D. team involved her in a myriad of tasks. "I always said having a degree in communicative disorders is a perfect degree for a corporate career," Welty said. "We had to teach ourselves about what organizational development was, socio-technical systems, leadership training, strategy development and process improvement. It was just kind of a new way of doing work and a new way of organizing a business."

Welty and the team worked to implement new incentive pay programs that fit the organizational development model. "It was just a new feel," she said, "and we went out and learned just as much as we could, and then we applied it to the organization. We did a lot of leadership training, emphasized what's it like to be a leader in this new world. There was a lot of reorganizing of work flows, a lot of looking at process flows. There was a lot of work with top management teams in formulating a strategy for the new world we would be entering into. It was very diverse."

In 1992, Al Hodnik was named co-leader of the O.D. team effort with Welty. Hodnik was the son of a longtime Minnesota Power employee, Ralph Hodnik, of Aurora. His father, who retired in 1978, helped Al find summer work at the Syl Laskin plant while he was in high school and attending the University of Minnesota. In 1981, he had just earned his degree and intended to attend the William Mitchell School of Law in the fall of 1982. His plans were to work for a year in the Twin Cities to save enough money for law school.

In March 1982, Hodnik received a phone call from Herb Moeller, manager at the Laskin plant. There was an opening at the plant. Was Hodnik interested in a full-time job?

Hodnik accepted the offer, and he and his wife, a Gilbert native, decided to make the Iron Range their home. Ironically, Hodnik's time on the east end of the Iron Range was cut short by economic conditions. The collapse of the taconite industry caused Minnesota Power to cut back on generation.

"I was laid off from Laskin by the fall of that year," Hodnik said, "and I ended up transferring over to Boswell Energy Center. I worked in the environmental area at Boswell until 1985. That's when Lake Superior Paper

Industries was coming on board, and the Hibbard plant was reactivated. I took my old job back at Laskin when people transferred down to take the Hibbard jobs. So I had some choppy times early on."

In 1990, Local 31 of the International Brotherhood of Electrical Workers—Hodnik's union—asked if he'd be interested in joining the O.D. team. Hodnik agreed and little more than a year later, he was named co-leader of the team. Hodnik subsequently "led the entire group by myself while I was still a member of Local 31, which at the time was somewhat of an anomaly for this Company."

Hodnik joined the Minnesota Power management team in 1994 when he was asked to return as plant manager of the Laskin Energy Center. Looking back, he considered his participation in the O.D. effort one of the high points of his career "because in many ways the O.D. effort broke down the way we used to behave. It was really the advent period of the notion of mission, vision, values and strategy."

Minnesota Power and the IBEW have been partners since 1937.

Hodnik noted that O.D. wasn't always an easy concept to sell in the plants. "Naturally in the beginning," he said, "it was met with somewhat of a feeling of skepticism. There was a lot of fear at the time because we were coming on the heels of a difficult situation with the taconite industry in the mid-1980s. There was the specter of deregulation, and I think O.D. initially was viewed largely as an effort to downsize, to eliminate the union, to lay people off, to change jobs and sort of break things apart. So we had that sort of current to run against. Then we also had the heavy layer of supervision in the plants. We had gone through the only strike in the Company's history in 1981. There had been some erosion in trust."

That short-lived 1981 strike had perhaps been more symptomatic of rank and file concern with the effect that inflation was having on paychecks. Minnesota Power was one of dozens of electric utilities that experienced the only strike in their history between 1979 and 1982. IBEW militancy in the period could be traced to frustration with economic circumstances rather than working conditions.

But by the 1990s, employees in the Company's power plants could see evidence that Minnesota Power and the electric utility industry were dramatically changing, Hodnik said. Technology and computerization were having a major impact, and as a result the plants were producing more kilowatt-hours with fewer people.

Hodnik noted that by the early 21st century, close to half the personnel manning the Company's power plants were expected to retire by 2010. They were likely to be replaced with a labor force with a different set of skills than an earlier generation of power plant workers.

"The type of worker who actually comes to the table today is armed differently," Hodnik said. "They're much more computer savvy. They're much more capable of dealing with electronics, keyboarding, doing laser alignment, precision maintenance on pumps and equipment—practices that 25 to 30 years ago may not even have been heard of, let alone talked about and implemented."

Welty pointed out that O.D. was perhaps most important for opening up communications channels within Minnesota Power. "I think people don't want to call it O.D., but I see it everywhere today," she said. "We just don't use those initials. What I see is the result of a lot of communications training, a lot of seeking to understand other people, their situations and how to work better with them. We took more than 1,000 employees through special training that helped people to communicate better with each other. That was major."

Florida Water and Land

An indication of how much Minnesota Power was changing came in the early 1990s when the Duluth utility's diversification initiative acquired a Florida land company and an Indiana-based automobile auction firm.

Planned unit developments, like this residential community in Lee County, Florida, fueled much of the growth in the Sunshine State during the 1980s and 1990s.

The initial acquisition of Florida land assets occurred in 1991 when Topeka Group, Minnesota Power's diversification subsidiary, made an offer to purchase the stock of Lehigh Utilities, Inc., a fast-growing residential development in Lee County just east of Fort Myers, Florida. The utility served about 10,000 customers with water, sewer, LP gas and garbage service. The water and sewer business of Lehigh Utilities seemed like a natural fit with the 160,000 water and wastewater customers already served by Southern States Utilities (SSU). But the proposed Florida acquisition soon became something other than a typical utility expansion.

Lehigh Acres was a development with a 40-year history. Originally a cattle ranch owned by Chicago businessman Lee Ratner, the property had been developed for residential purposes in the mid-1950s. Ratner and his partners formed Lee County Land and Title Company. During the 1960s and 1970s, when better known developers such as Del Webb and the Mackle Brothers were making their marks on Southwest Florida, Lehigh Acres was developed in fits and starts by a succession of owners, including the Catholic Diocese of Austin, Texas.

The Lehigh Acres acquisition included an 18-hole golf course near Fort Myers.

By the mid-1980s, the renamed Lehigh Corporation was acquired by Security Savings and Loan Association of Scottsdale, Arizona. Security Savings and Loan was one of the victims of the S&L shakeout of the mid-1980s, and it failed in 1987.

"We first went after Lehigh Utilities in 1989," said Donnie Crandell. "Our initial interest was only the utilities."

At the time, ownership of Lehigh Corporation's estimated $100 million in assets passed from the Federal Savings and Loan Insurance Corp. to the Federal Deposit Insurance Corporation, and then to the Resolution Trust Corp. (RTC). RTC was resolute about selling Lehigh Acres as a complete package.

By that time, Lehigh Corporation's assets, in addition to the utilities, included more than 13,000 single home lots, a hotel, two golf courses, a printing business, a building supply firm and a home-building business. Lehigh Utilities served 10,000 homes and 30,000 residents. With the platted single home lots and additional developable acreage, Lehigh was expected to be a community of more than 120,000 people by 2020.

Crandell convinced Minnesota Power management to recruit several

Florida real estate developers to join with Topeka Group in a joint venture offering for all of Lehigh Acres. Crandell convinced Dick McMahon, a Miami developer, and Frank Ford of the Ford Property Trust in Volusia County to join Minnesota Power in a bid for Lehigh Acres. The bid came in at $62 million.

"Somebody at the S&L showed our bid to General Development Corporation, and they bid $1 million more—$63 million," Crandell said. GDC, however, went bankrupt itself before it could close the Lehigh Acres purchase.

The Resolution Trust Corp., tasked by Congress with liquidating billions of dollars of distressed real estate in its portfolio, still wanted to unload Lehigh Acres. Crandell tracked down the RTC staffer responsible for the Security S&L land portfolio and asked if the property was still for sale. It was.

"We negotiated a $40 million deal," he said, "down $22 million from our first offer. We got much better terms than the original deal."

In early July 1991, the RTC elected to take Minnesota Power's offer. Topeka Group assigned Lehigh Utilities to SSU. To handle day-to-day operations of the Lehigh non-utility business, Topeka Group recruited Bill Livingston as president of the new Minnesota Power subsidiary. Livingston, a veteran of nearly 20 years with Deltona Corp. and Gulfstream Land and Development Corporation, was named to oversee development of the already platted lots at Lehigh. Livingston quickly pared the size of the Lehigh Corporation staff and began to lay the foundations of what would become profitable Minnesota Power Florida land holdings.

"The market really started to turn up in 1991," Crandell explained. "We started to collect a lot of money on the outstanding mortgages. Bill Livingston sold the golf course in 1992. We got the golf course and other property at the manufacturer's cost. Our plan was to sell at wholesale and make our profit and let the developers make a profit on the retail side. We were always business to business in land sales. We didn't get into the vertical side of the business."

Acquiring ADESA

If Minnesota Power's foray into Florida land development surprised the normally staid world occupied by electric utility analysts, the Duluth Company's next investment left the analyst community in total shock.

In early 1995, Minnesota Power announced it had agreed to purchase

80 percent of the outstanding stock of ADESA, an Indianapolis-based automobile auction company. Minnesota Power agreed to pay $167 million for the 80 percent of ADESA's outstanding stock.

The ADESA acquisition had been in the works for several years. 1993 was a difficult year for northeastern Minnesota and Minnesota Power. National Steel Pellet Company at Keewatin closed for much of the year as competitive pressures continued to impact the region's taconite industry. Paper prices skidded to the lowest ever recorded, and Minnesota Power's ReachAll subsidiary continued to report operating losses. Minnesota Power had acquired ReachAll, a Duluth-based manufacturer of hydraulic boom vehicles primarily used in utility work, to keep jobs from leaving northeastern Minnesota. Higher than expected costs at Lehigh Corporation and inability to recover Florida water expenses by initiating rate increases at SSU resulted in 1993 earnings of $2.20 a share, Minnesota Power's lowest EPS since 1984.

ADESA personnel entertain a bid on a late model used car at the auto auction company's Indianapolis facility.

Wall Street was quick to react. A wave of sell orders buffeted Minnesota Power common shares through the latter half of 1993 and most of 1994. The stock price was bolstered no matter what the Company did during the ensuing period. And the problems with the stalled Florida rate case and the mushrooming expenses at Lehigh Corporation signaled that the vast majority of Minnesota Power's business, although diversified, was for the most part diversified into water and wastewater treatment utilities.

In early 1994, Sandbulte instructed Topeka Group staffers to widen their search for the Company's next diversified venture. Topeka Group's Donnie Crandell went back to an old friend, Stuart Utgaard of St. Paul. Utgaard operated Enterprise Investments, a firm that uncovered potential acquisitions for firms in the market, such as Minnesota Power. A decade before, Utgaard had located UTI for Jack McDonald, Crandell and Topeka Group.

"We wanted a business with manageable risk," Sandbulte told shareholders early in 1995, "and the potential for growth and returns higher than those of a typical utility business. We looked at firms in 25 to 30 different industries, beginning with utility-related businesses and then gradually broadening our scope."

What Sandbulte and Minnesota Power were searching for was the third leg of the three-legged stool. "The three-legged tripod or stool—a metaphor for three financially supportive business units I've referred to in the past—has two legs that are utility water and electric, and the third is one for which we have been searching for some time," Sandbulte explained to employees in 1995.

During the first six months of 1994, Utgaard examined utility-related businesses, including international electric utilities that were discarded because of their inherent political risk. Next to be investigated were oil and gas exploration firms, which were rejected because they were too cyclical. Manufacturing was briefly looked at and set aside because it was so capital intensive. Several title insurance firms were investigated, but the cyclical nature of their business and the industry's tie to interest rates quickly disqualified them from contention.

Workers erect a logo on the side of the building housing ADESA's Boston Auto Auction.

In mid-1994, the search firm brought ADESA to the attention of Topeka Group and Minnesota Power. ADESA was North America's third-largest auto auction company, with headquarters in Indianapolis, Indiana, and 16 auction locations nationwide. The company provided a venue for sellers—typically fleet and lease companies, rental car firms, auto manufacturers and automobile importers. Buyers typically were car dealers.

Sandbulte recalled being initially skeptical about ADESA. "I said, 'Wait a minute, auto auction, I don't think so,'" he remembered his first impression. "That doesn't sound like the kind of business that we would be in. I was thinking guys with big cigars and big plaid sports jackets and wide ties."

Sandbulte and Jack McDonald met with Mike Hockett, Larry Wechter and Jerry Williams, three of the principals in ADESA, in Indianapolis during the summer of 1994. What Sandbulte and McDonald saw convinced them that ADESA was worth pursuing. ADESA sold more than 400,000 vehicles in 1994. The automobile auction company made its money through auction fees and auxiliary services including auto reconditioning, dealer financing and transportation services. In 1994, the firm's net income was $7.8 million on gross revenues of just under $95 million.

Service, Redistribution and Finance

Mike Hockett, the Indianapolis entrepreneur who in 1979 started ADESA with a partner, described his auto auction firm in 1991 as "a young, growing company." Indeed, the company was growing so fast that ADESA more than doubled the number of autos it sold at auction from 1992 to 1994.

Hockett grew up in the automobile business. His father was a well-known Hoosier car dealer during the 1950s and 1960s. Initially a teacher and coach after graduating from Indianapolis' Butler University, Hockett started selling cars at area dealers in the mid-1960s. His father had purchased 51 percent of an auto auction firm in Indianapolis, and Mike Hockett joined the business in 1966. In 1968, Hockett's father sold the auction firm to Atlanta-based Cox Communications. Mike Hockett worked for Cox for most of the next 11 years.

In 1980, Hockett and a partner founded Automobile Dealers Exchange (ADE) on the southeast side of Indianapolis. ADE acquired auto auctions in the Midwest and Mid-South before the partner bought out Hockett in the mid-1980s. Hockett then purchased another auto auction in the Hoosier capital city. That became ADESA, and Hockett quickly grew his new company with the purchase of auction sites in the Great Lakes states and Canada. In 1992, Hockett took ADESA public.

When Minnesota Power came looking in 1995, Hockett realized that the Duluth utility was potentially an excellent match. "The only thing that constrains us from further growth is capital," he said in mid-1995. "And our greatest growth opportunity is in finance."

For his part, Sandbulte saw similar opportunities. "This acquisition may have little to do with utilities," he told employees, "but it has everything to do with our profit strategy. In our strategic plan, we've always identified financial services as a component of our Company. I consider the securities portfolio and Capital Re as financial service businesses.

"There's a financial services part to ADESA, although I'd categorize ADESA at this time as more of a corporate service business than a financial service business. I've likened it to a stock or commodity exchange where buyers and sellers are brought together and the person operating the exchange—us—is not the vehicle's owner, but rather provides services for the buyers and sellers. It's a niche service business for the automotive industry, which is huge. ADESA is a large player in this niche."

Minnesota Power's board of directors approved the merger in mid-February 1995, and ADESA shareholders signaled their assent in April. The next year, Minnesota Power exercised its option to purchase the remaining shares held by ADESA management, giving the Company complete control of ADESA. By then, ADESA had grown to 24 auction sites nationwide and was moving more than 600,000 vehicles a year through its facilities.

Sandbulte's biggest disappointment was the inability of Wall Street to understand the ADESA acquisition. "I remember going to New York with Larry Wechter," Sandbulte said, "and this was shortly after we announced the deal in 1996. The analysts who were there were mostly utility analysts, and they were kind of befuddled, their jaws were clenched and their teeth were on edge a little bit. They were asking themselves, 'How in the heck are we going to analyze this Company?' And we were talking about the fact that through thick and through thin in the used car business, people are buying and selling cars all the time, whether they're buying more new ones or not. 'It's not nearly as cyclical as you might think,' we told them."

During the nearly 10 years that Minnesota Power owned ADESA, Wall Street never understood the concept of an electric utility owning an auto auction company. But the analysts did understand that Minnesota Power operated one of the more sophisticated investment departments in all of American industry.

CHAPTER 12 Riding the Bull Market

I n the 1990s, America rode one of the more exuberant bull markets since the go-go days of the conglomerates in the late 1950s and early 1960s. The almost uninterrupted upward surge of the stock market during the decade quadrupled the value of the influential Dow Jones Industrial Average (DJIA) by January 1, 2000.

Minnesota Power shareholders profited from the 1990s bull market. An investment portfolio that chairman, president and CEO Arend Sandbulte and his staff had begun putting together in the mid-1980s contributed double-digit returns to the utility's bottom line during the 1990s. Returns from the investment portfolio helped fund Minnesota Power's acquisition of Florida land properties and ADESA after 1990.

The investment strategy did not appear as much of a good idea in the late 1980s. The Dow Jones

The stately entrance to Wall Street's New York Stock Exchange is a reminder that Minnesota Power has an obligation to its shareholders that dates back to the founding of the Company.

had hit a record 2,722 in August 1987 and promised to break the magical 3,000 mark by the end of the year. But the stock market crash of October 19, 1987 wiped out 23 percent of the value of the DJIA in one trading session. Stocks dropped 508 points on what brokers soon took to calling Black Monday. The percentage loss was greater than the 12.8 percent plunge that started the Great Depression on October 28, 1929.

But unlike 1929, the system quickly righted itself. Federal Reserve Board Chairman Alan Greenspan calmed jittery markets when he said that the Fed would be a lender of last resort to the nation's stock exchanges if the situation worsened. The market drifted through the remainder of the year, but the economy continued growing. By 1989, the DJIA recovered the ground lost on Black Monday. In January 1990, the Dow stood at 2,810, about three percent higher than it had been just over two years before when the market crashed.

From there, the economy rocketed upward. Impelled by a boom in technology stocks, the market turned into the first "superbull" in history. The Dow crossed 3,000 in the spring of 1991 and 3,500 two springs later. It passed 4,000 in early 1995, 5,000 later that year and 6,000 in October 1996. It sometimes seemed as if the sky was the limit. The market climbed above 7,000 in early 1997, 8,000 in July and 9,000 in the spring of 1998. The magical number of 10,000 was surpassed on March 29, 1999. A mere 35 days later, the Dow climbed past 11,000.

Never in history had the markets ascended so far, so fast. And thanks to Sandbulte and the investment portfolio, Minnesota Power shareholders had been deriving benefits from the start.

'You Can't Go Wrong Buying Municipal Bonds'

The genesis of Minnesota Power's investment portfolio can be traced to 1980, when the utility had just completed construction of Clay Boswell Unit 4. "We had wound down the construction budget substantially," explained Sandbulte. "So we started generating substantial amounts of cash, depreciation and retained earnings."

The economic fallout of President Jimmy Carter's administration included a prime interest rate of about 20 percent in the early 1980s. "When we were investing," Sandbulte said, "we could buy municipal bonds, tax exempt, yielding about 12 percent to 14 percent. I said, 'We can't go wrong buying good quality municipal bonds, tax exempt.'"

The Company's purchase of municipal bonds started in 1982 and continued through the mid-1980s. "So after the municipal well sort of ran dry, mostly because of availability, then we started buying preferred stocks in other utilities because there was a dividend exclusion," Sandbulte explained. "You didn't have to pay tax on the dividends if you bought them as another utility. There was an exclusion." Dennis Hollingsworth and Jerry Dodd in the Company's treasury department became the utility's investment experts.

"We bought leveraged preferred where you could deduct interest," Sandbulte said. "We set up trusts where you could deduct the interest in the trust for taxes, but you could use the dividend exclusion to protect or shelter the dividends. It was really a good situation until that law got changed. At one time, we had over $400 million involved in the portfolio, mostly in utility preferreds. But, meanwhile, we were keeping our powder dry and looking for opportunities in diversification."

Duluth native Jim Vizanko earned his undergraduate degree at the University of Minnesota Duluth (UMD) and then taught high school math in the Twin Ports. In 1977, Vizanko was considering moving to the Twin Cities to pursue an M.B.A. when he answered a job opening at Minnesota Power. Vizanko was hired and went to work for Dave Gartzke, who had been one of his instructors at UMD.

Vizanko's initial title was assistant forecasting and economics analyst, and he became chief financial officer in 2001. "I was doing load forecast, primarily for the taconite customers, and residential load," Vizanko said. "The Company was basically an electric utility only then. Most of the people hired in the 1970s were building Boswell Unit 4 at the time, so the Company was growing in size."

Vizanko recalled that a "lot of the people were very young, just started in the business. They didn't have a lot of service, versus now."

Vizanko worked with Dennis Hollingsworth on the Company's investment portfolio for much of the 1980s and 1990s. He pointed out that the utility's financial role "has certainly changed over the years. I was very involved in the investment portfolio for many years. That grew from nothing to over $400 million. And then to zero a couple years ago when we liquidated it."

Another element of the portfolio was the Company's investment in Capital Re, a reinsurance vehicle. "We put money in Capital Re, and then that merged with ACE, another reinsurance firm," Vizanko said. "We sold ACE stock. Over that entire period of time, we purchased Baukol-Noonan (BNI), we purchased real estate, bought and sold the water businesses in Florida, and got into the paper mill, Lake Superior Paper Industries (LSPI), with Pentair. And we added a recycling facility to that and then sold it."

To Vizanko, the biggest change in utility financing during the past 30 years has been the buying and selling of businesses. "We've certainly done a huge amount of that and a lot of financing, too. We've raised a great deal of money to buy some of these businesses and, over time, sold a lot of common stock to buy these things."

Vizanko noted that the most significant difference between the 1980s and the early 2000s is Minnesota Power's real estate portfolio. "Basically, the utility is of similar size today from a megawatt-hour stance compared to what we were 20 years ago," Vizanko said. "But now we have our real estate business in Florida, as well as BNI and the generating station we purchased at Taconite Harbor. By and large, that core utility business has remained stable. We bought and sold things over the years, and what's left now is the core utility plus the real estate business."

Vizanko announced his retirement from ALLETE in June 2006 after a nearly 30-year career with the Company. Named treasurer in 1993 and CFO in 2001, Vizanko intended to stay busy in retirement. Following his retirement in the fall of 2006, Vizanko joined the faculty of the University of Minnesota Duluth, his alma mater.

"During his almost 29 years with the Company, Jim has made a huge contribution to the Company's diversification effort and its outstanding financial performance," said Donald J. Shippar, ALLETE's chairman, president and chief executive officer.

Robert J. Adams was another Duluth native who joined the Company's finance team and made strong contributions to diversification efforts in the 1980s and 1990s. Like Vizanko, Adams earned his accounting degree from UMD. While attending school, he interned for a year in the then Minnesota Power internal audit department.

Following graduation in 1985, Adams worked for McGladrey & Pullen, a local accounting firm. In 1986, Gerry Van Tassel of the Company's corporate finance group called Adams and asked him to interview for a position with the Company.

"I interviewed with Dave Gartzke," Adams said. "At the time, he was the director of rates and financial planning and analysis. He told me about Arend Sandbulte's goal of generating half of the Company's earnings from diversified entities."

Financing ADESA

Perhaps the most significant role played by Minnesota Power's portfolio came in 1995 when the Duluth utility financed the $167 million purchase of ADESA, the Indianapolis-based automobile auction firm.

"At the time, the Company wasn't looking to get into the automotive business," explained Herb Minke, a business analyst who joined corporate development in 1993. "They were looking for a business that had good, strong organic growth. They wanted something specifically that was growing in excess of what the electric business was growing. They wanted a business that produced a good, solid, strong cash flow. They wanted a business that wasn't necessarily capital intensive, one that could be used to balance electric utility operations in Minnesota."

Minke, who arrived in Duluth from the Toledo office of Deloitte & Touche, said the ADESA acquisition was to be financed from Minnesota

Power's investment portfolio. "The idea was to take the cash that had been sitting on the balance sheet generated by the investment portfolio, the internal investment portfolio that had generated such significant profits over the years, and put that out into operating capital to get a little bit better rate of return," Minke noted.

Minke recalled that ADESA wasn't a top

ADESA's auction in Boston was just one of dozens the Indianapolis automobile auction firm opened or expanded in the 1990s.

acquisition candidate until the corporate development group did a strategic analysis on the diversified businesses Minnesota Power was investigating.

"If you look at the list of projects we had going on at the time, it wasn't the top prospect in the Company," Minke explained. "We were looking at partnering with an oil and gas company to buy some water, oil and gas assets. We were looking at coal mining businesses and also were looking at environmental service businesses. The ADESA project was one that a lot of people felt wasn't going to be the primary candidate to look at."

But when Minke and the corporate development group screened potential acquisitions for compliance with strategic goals, ADESA consistently showed up high on the list. "And it showed up for a number of reasons," Minke said. "One was the cash flow generated by ADESA was very high. It also was a small company that could be expanded as well, to be added on to investment capital and provide growth for the Company."

Minke, who was named director of accounting in 2005, said financing ADESA was one of his proudest moments with Minnesota Power. "I was very lucky that I sat in on the board meeting when the board decided to acquire ADESA, and I sat in on the board meeting when the board decided to spin them off," he said.

In between, ADESA contributed to the growth of Minnesota Power's investment portfolio. "In 2004 the board decided to spin ADESA off to shareholders," said Dave Gartzke, who later moved to Indianapolis to head the automobile auction company. "ADESA had been turned around. It was growing leaps and bounds. The automobile salvage business was beginning to take off. Automotive Finance Corporation (AFC) had grown to a level no one had ever anticipated. ADESA was becoming a behemoth, but it was still misunderstood by Wall Street."

Double-Digit Returns

Minnesota Power's adroit use of investment capital to diversify proved to be a financial windfall for the Company during the late 1990s and early 2000s. By 2001, the utility's investment portfolio, including its position in Capital Re and its investment in diversification opportunities in the automotive auction business, water and wastewater treatment, and Florida land development were returning anywhere from seven percent to 10 percent a year.

Duluth and northeastern Minnesota media report Minnesota Power's announcement that it is changing the Company's name to ALLETE to reflect that the Duluth firm has become "more than Minnesota, more than power."

Even more impressive, the utility's total shareholder return (TSR)—a measure of the utility's stock price and dividend performance—had been among the industry's leaders for more than two decades. Annual TSR averaged 17 percent a year between 1980 and 2001. From 1996 to 2001, Minnesota Power's TSR averaged 19 percent a year. And from 1999 to 2001, when ADESA began to become a dominant force in the automotive auction industry, TSR averaged 28 percent a year.

The Minnesota Power investment portfolio and strategy had been assembled and defined by Arend Sandbulte during the 1980s. But the results of the strategy would be most obvious during the late 1990s. By then, Sandbulte's successors would be at the helm of ALLETE, the new name adopted by Minnesota Power to reflect its diversified businesses. The electric utility would continue to operate as Minnesota Power.

13 More than Minnesota,
More than Power

After presiding over an era of change unprecedented in the utility's
nearly 90-year history, Arend Sandbulte elected to step down from
the day-to-day leadership of Minnesota Power. In 1995, he told
the utility's Board of Directors that he wanted to relinquish his role as
president and chief executive officer. During a transition period, Sandbulte
would serve as chairman of the board until his retirement.

Sandbulte's years at the helm of Minnesota Power were truly
momentous. During the six years since he succeeded Jack Rowe as
chairman, Sandbulte had put an indelible stamp on a transformed
Minnesota Power.

He would be remembered for three principal achievements. Sandbulte
accelerated Minnesota Power's diversification initiative, acquiring
ADESA and positioning Minnesota Power for growth in the Florida land
development business. He assembled the investment portfolio that allowed
Minnesota Power to acquire a host of diversified subsidiaries, and he
instituted an innovative organizational development program that helped
Minnesota Power employees cope with the dramatic pace of change.

Sandbulte agreed to serve one year as chairman of the Minnesota
Power Board of Directors and an additional two years on the board, as he
transitioned into full retirement. Unforeseen circumstances dictated that
Sandbulte actually served six years on the Minnesota Power Board, retiring
in 2002.

Looking back on his career with Minnesota Power, Sandbulte was
proudest of the financial legacy left to his successors. In 2004, he asked
then President and CEO David Gartzke to calculate what the value of a
$1,000 investment in Minnesota Power stock in 1980 was worth nearly a
quarter-century later. "It just happened my sister-in-law had bought stock
in about 1980," Sandbulte explained. "So Dave had his financial people
figure it out, and the $1,000 invested in 1980, 23 years later in 2003 was
worth $44,000."

That price included the dividend reinvestment plus growth in the
stock, a 17-percent compounded annual rate of return. "And if you look at
the stock market," Sandbulte said, "there are very few companies that can
produce that kind of a return for that long a period."

A Leader from Outside

When the Minnesota Power board announced the Company's new president to succeed Sandbulte in 1995, the choice was somewhat of a surprise. Edwin L. Russell was the first outsider named to the post at the Duluth utility since Clay Boswell arrived at then MP&L from Utah Power & Light Company in the 1940s.

Befitting a company that had become increasingly diversified since the mid-1980s, Russell also was the first non-utility chief executive in the Company's history. Russell, then 50, joined Minnesota Power in May 1995 following a quarter-century of experience in non-regulated business. Immediately prior to joining Minnesota Power, Russell was group vice president at J.M. Huber Corp., a broadly diversified manufacturing and natural resources company headquartered in Edison, New Jersey. Russell earned a B.A. degree in international government from Bowdoin College in Maine, as well as an M.B.A. from the Harvard Business School of Business Administration.

Bob Mars served on the search committee that selected Sandbulte's successor. He noted that the board of directors was determined to select the best possible person for the job.

The first thing the search committee did was "take a look at the inside and see who worked for the Company that could handle the diversified activities," Mars said. "And it was already pretty diversified then."

Mars noted that the board's decision to look outside was not a comment on the qualifications of the internal candidates. He said that Russell was one of several candidates Minnesota Power's executive search firm recruited.

"The whole concept of diversification and the wide geography involved is a unique management experience," Mars explained. "The businesses that you are diversified in are all quite different, and Ed Russell just had a world of experience in successfully managing outside companies that were located in different places with different management. When we got done with the search, it was a given if he'd accept the job."

Introduced at the annual meeting of shareholders in 1996, Russell promised "a sense of strong purpose and optimism for the future." At that annual meeting in May 1996, Russell was named to the post of chief executive officer. Later that day, the former New Jersey resident was elected chairman of the board to replace Sandbulte.

Russell was involved in two of the utility's more significant transactions during the 1990s. In June 1995, Minnesota Power closed on an 80-percent acquisition of Indianapolis-based ADESA, a total corporate investment of more than $167 million. With plans to auction as many as 500,000 vehicles at its 16 North American auction facilities, ADESA was expected to immediately begin making significant contributions to Minnesota Power's bottom line.

At the same time it acquired ADESA, Minnesota Power announced the sale of its interests in Lake Superior Paper Industries (LSPI) and Superior Recycled Fiber Industries, Inc. The sale to Consolidated Paper, Inc. of Wisconsin Rapids, Wisconsin, was completed for $118 million, plus the assumption of some debt and subject to certain lease obligations. The sale had been expected for several years. Since announcing the construction of LSPI more than a decade before, Minnesota Power always had stressed that the paper mill in West Duluth represented an investment in the economic development of the Twin Ports and northeastern Minnesota and was not part of the utility's diversification initiative.

Russell also was involved in the somewhat more difficult exercise of Minnesota Power's option to acquire the remaining 20 percent of ADESA in 1996. Mike Hockett, the Indianapolis-based founder of the automobile auction firm, and other members of the ADESA management team, continued to own 20 percent of the ADESA stock.

"Mike Hockett was a good, fair man," Sandbulte said. "He had grown up in the car business. He was an idea man who had a lightbulb idea every so often."

Russell asked Sandbulte to go to Indianapolis with him and try to work out an advance buyout of the remaining 20 percent of ADESA stock. ADESA management and investors, Jerry Williams and Larry Wechter, also attended the summer 1997 meeting. Russell and Hockett quickly reached agreement on the transfer of the final block of 20 percent of ADESA common stock to Minnesota Power.

"And so in about 20 to 30 minutes, we had a deal to buy out the remainder of Mike's stock," Sandbulte said, "and that's how the transition of management occurred at ADESA."

Following the negotiations, Minnesota Power named a Canadian veteran of the auto auction firm to replace Hockett as president. Jim Hallett, who had founded auto auction facilities in Ottawa, Ontario, and Halifax, Nova Scotia, was serving as president of ADESA's Canadian operations when Russell asked him to move to Indianapolis to head the Minnesota Power subsidiary.

New Faces on the Management Team

Russell's early tenure led to several significant management changes at Minnesota Power and its diversification subsidiaries. Since Russell lacked electric utility management experience, the Board named a seasoned veteran of the utility's core electric operation as the new president of MP Electric.

Robert D. "Bob" Edwards was a native of southern Minnesota and a 1966 graduate of Mankato State College with a degree in business administration and math. Edwards joined Price Waterhouse, a CPA firm in Minneapolis, in 1967 and worked with the accounting firm until 1976. "Ironically," he said, "one of the first clients I had with Price Waterhouse was the Minnesota Power assignment. In January 1967, one of my first assignments was as a member of the MP audit team."

Edwards' progression up the Minnesota Power corporate ladder was sure and steady. During much of his career, he worked with budgeting and accounting issues. He was named corporate controller in 1976, a vice president of the Company in 1983, and a group vice president and chief operating officer 10 years later.

In the summer of 1995, shortly after Russell had taken the reins of Minnesota Power, the new president reached back to New Jersey for a management hire at Southern States Utilities. John Cirello was named president and chief executive officer of SSU. He replaced SSU CFO Scott Vierima, who had been interim CEO since Bert Phillips retired the previous year.

Cirello, who earned a doctorate at Rutgers University, came to SSU from Environmental Energy Services, Inc., a Bound Brook, New Jersey, environmental consulting firm he headed. Cirello previously had held executive positions with several New Jersey-based environmental management firms, as well as served as an assistant professor and instructor at Rutgers University.

Two other Minnesota Power managers who would play key roles in the utility's continuing evolution during the late 1990s and early 21st century assumed new positions in 1994. David Gartzke, the utility's treasurer since 1988, was named senior vice president and chief financial officer. Donnie Crandell, one of the architects of the Company's diversification strategy, was named senior vice president of corporate development.

Changes in the Core Business

For Bob Edwards and the staff of MP Electric, change was in the air in the mid-1990s. Following more than a decade of diversification activity, Minnesota Power's core electric business accounted for less than half the Company's assets.

"The mid-1990s were a difficult time for the electric industry and electric companies in general because it was approaching the peak of customer choice and all the activity around the country in terms of open access," Edwards said. "And we continued to have a very high concentration of sales to large industrial companies with whom we had long-term take-or-pay contracts. Most of those contracts were expiring in the mid-1990s. The Minntac contract was our largest contract, and it was expiring in 1996. They were very vocal that they were going to leave the Company at that time."

MP Electric took several steps to make the utility more competitive in an increasingly deregulated environment. In 1996, Minnesota Power began to integrate a system of key account management, in which Minnesota Power marketing personnel were assigned to work closely with their counterparts at large industrial customers.

"We had designated people as key account managers," explained Margaret Hodnik, one of the first key account managers. "They were asked to really understand what's going on with the customer's business at that site. They were also expected to know what's going on in the

Key Account Manager Jeff Hoyum confers with Tom Dostal at United Taconite over ways to implement energy savings.

industry, what kind of influences are coming in that will help or hurt their customers' businesses. Key account managers asked customers questions. What do they need? How do they feel about us? Do they understand the contract? What kind of energy service could they use beyond what we are currently offering that would most benefit their operation? How can we dovetail our energy service offering so that they can increase production, we can increase sales, and everybody can benefit?"

Eric Norberg, a Tower-Soudan native with more than 20 years of experience in power delivery, credited the key account management program with helping taconite customers become more competitive in the late 1990s.

"We needed to change," he said, "and we did. That was one of the things that made me real proud about Minnesota Power. The marketing people couldn't deliver a kilowatt-hour or respond to an outage, but it had to be the employees at Minnesota Power who embraced change. We did a lot of communication with the employees on the importance of why we needed to work with our customers differently, and it worked. We entered into a landmark 11-year contract with USX that set the pattern for many of our other customers. That was in 1997."

Norberg noted that "the principles of key account management are very ingrained in this organization. And we have good relationships with our largest customers."

In the spring of 1996, Minnesota Power launched the MPEX division to engage in wholesale power marketing and energy exchange under Mike Critchley, a popular veteran of the utility's dispatch operations.

The primary mission of the new entrepreneurial division and Critchley, its president, was to target power delivery to investor-owned utilities, municipalities, electric cooperatives and government agencies in Minnesota, Iowa, Montana, Nebraska, the Dakotas, Wisconsin and adjacent Canadian provinces. With interconnections to both Ontario Hydro and Manitoba Hydro, MPEX could deliver low-cost electric power to its customers.

"It's logical that we formalize our experience and capabilities in power marketing and energy exchange by establishing a new division with its own identity," Bob Edwards said in describing the formation of MPEX, adding that the division would capitalize on the utility's 25-year reputation in power marketing.

MPEX eventually formed a power supply alliance with Great River Energy, a generation and transmission cooperative headquartered in Elk River, Minnesota. The alliance, which later created Split Rock Energy in the Twin Cities, was designed to combine power supply assets and customer loads for the rapidly evolving power pool operations in the Upper Midwest.

ALLETE

The rapid diversification and growth of Minnesota Power during the 1990s created a company that was no longer just an electric service provider for 140,000 residential and about a dozen large industrial customers in northeastern Minnesota. By 1999, MP represented 43 percent of the parent firm's assets. ADESA and the automotive subsidiaries comprised 29 percent of Minnesota Power's assets, while the Company's water operations and investment portfolios represented 14 percent apiece.

The increasingly diversified asset base led the Minnesota Power Board of Directors to unveil a new identification at the dawn of the 21st century. On September 1, 2000, brokers at the New York Stock Exchange watched as a new ticker symbol—ALE—scrolled across the big board. The symbol signified a change of name. After almost 95 years as Minnesota Power, the Duluth-based company had changed its name to ALLETE.

Workers install the ALLETE logo on the Company's headquarters at 30 West Superior Street in Duluth.

"Our new name reinforces our continuing transformation to a multi-service company with diverse strengths in basic necessities, such as cars, electricity, water and real estate," Chairman, President and CEO Ed Russell told shareholders.

Although its assets were shrinking in comparison to some of ALLETE's other business lines, MP enjoyed renewed growth in the late 1990s and early 2000s. The diversification of the regional economy had been jump-started by tourism initiatives in Duluth and the Iron Range, by the expansion of UMD, and by the growth of Cirrus Design, a Duluth-based airplane manufacturer. But the Arrowhead economy surged in the late 1990s because of the strength of its iron mining sector.

By 2000, the Mesabi Range iron ore industry had been downsized and re-engineered to supply the integrated steel industry on the Lower Great Lakes. The industry employed some 6,500 people year-round, and about another 1,000 to 1,500 people in corollary industries. The industry had recorded five of six production years above 40 million tons of pellets, essentially full production. In 2000, 54 of the 56 dry bulk carriers in the U.S. and Canadian Great Lakes fleets were in service. World prices for iron ore pellets were rising six percent to seven percent a year, and the U.S. spot price for pellets was $41.50 per long ton, up from $35 the year before.

The recovery of the Range taconite industry late in the decade led to several projects designed to strengthen MP's capacity situation. In 2000, MP agreed to purchase capacity from Great River Energy, its partner in Split Rock Energy. Great River Energy was in the process of building a new gas-fired generating plant at Lakefield in southwestern Minnesota.

The Lakefield Junction Project was a 480-megawatt peaking plant. It comprised six combustion turbines fueled by natural gas. MP's share of the project was 240 megawatts in 2001 and 2002, and 80 megawatts in 2003 and 2004.

Electric power growth wasn't constrained to Minnesota Power's service territory. In 1998, Wisconsin Governor Tommy Thompson reported that parts of the Badger State were critically short of electric power capacity and called on the state's utilities to help remedy the situation. In response, Wisconsin Public Service Corporation and MP announced plans to build a 345,000-volt transmission line from Wausau, Wisconsin, to the Arrowhead Substation near Duluth.

The planned 250-mile transmission line project was dubbed "PowerUp Wisconsin." Governor Thompson noted that the line "will go a long way toward assuring Wisconsin residents will have affordable energy while at the same time helping to improve electric reliability. In addition, it will help bring low-cost electricity into the state which is necessary to support economic growth and the creation of new jobs."

In December 1999, MP and Wisconsin Public Service submitted a two-volume, 1,400-page application for the transmission line project to the Public Service Commission of Wisconsin.

Enventis

ALLETE also was alert to the opportunities posed by the expansion of the Internet. In early 1998, the Company filed documents with the Minnesota Public Utilities Commission for its new telecommunications subsidiary, MP Telecom. MP President Bob Edwards noted that "the formation of MP Telecom as a distinct operating subsidiary signals our intent to more extensively compete in the rapidly evolving telecommunications industry. MP Telecom will become one of the major providers of large capacity, high quality fiber optic network services in the Upper Midwest."

Bob Adams, who had learned the diversification business from the inside-out working with Donnie Crandell in the late 1980s and early 1990s, was working for Bob Edwards in 1997, trying to leverage the electric utility's expertise into other potential profit centers.

"We had the opportunity to upgrade our old microwave system to a fiber-based system," Adams explained. "It just doesn't cost a lot more to invest in additional strands of fiber. It occurred to us that we could lease some of that capacity. So we did a business plan."

Dan Fahland, a technician with MP Telecom, inspects computerized switching equipment.

By December 1998, MP Telecom had completed a state-of-the-art fiber optic telecommunications network interconnecting the northern Minnesota communities of Duluth, Brainerd, Grand Rapids, Hibbing, Virginia and Eveleth. Capable of handling 20 gigabits of capacity, the system was designed to serve more than 250,000 Internet customers. MP Telecom's 1999 plans included connecting Ely, Aurora-Hoyt Lakes, Babbitt and other northeastern Minnesota communities, as well as expanding the network to the Twin Cities of Minneapolis-St. Paul.

Early in 1999, MP Telecom was chosen to provide telecommunications and data services for the Duluth Technology Village, then under construction at Lake Avenue and Superior Street. Later that year, MP Telecom began construction of a 208-mile fiber optic grid linking Winona, Rochester, Austin, Albert Lea, Owatonna, Faribault and Minneapolis. With activation of the southern route, MP Telecom would have more than 1,000 route miles of fiber optic network in Minnesota, effectively connecting three-quarters of the state's population.

"From 1997 to 2000," Adams explained, "we built one of the top three fiber networks in the state. In much of the northern sector of the system, we built along Minnesota Power's right-of-way, so that kept costs down. We were fully redundant, and we were leasing fiber to big-time telecommunications firms, including AT&T.

By 2000, much of the nation was glutted with fiber capacity. Long-term profitability was in question, but MP Telecom made a strategic decision to stay in the business. "We started looking at the installation and consolidation of Voice Over Internet Protocol (systems) for customers," Adams said. "We would literally get them set up inside the walls and outside the walls."

In July 2001, MP Telecom acquired Enventis, the premier VoIP integrator in Minnesota. The firm, founded in Plymouth in 1998, had $18 million in revenues in 2000. In 2002, the combined company reported $28 million in revenues. Three years later, in 2005, Enventis had nearly doubled its revenue stream to $50 million.

"We added people and expertise," Adams said. "We continued to build out the fiber network. Our system went as far east as Eau Claire, Wisconsin. By 2005, revenues were growing at a compound rate of 30 percent a year."

With growth at MP, ADESA, Enventis and its Florida real estate investment portfolio, ALLETE was well-positioned to face the challenges of the 21st century.

CHAPTER 14 A Utility for the Third Millennium

A LLETE faced some unexpected challenges in the early years of the 21st century. After enjoying substantial growth during the late 1990s, Minnesota's Mesabi Range taconite industry began the new millennium under a cloud of uncertainty as the nation's steel industry again restructured to meet global competition. Minnesota Power faced grassroots opposition from Wisconsin residents concerned about the Wausau to Duluth high-voltage transmission line. And Ed Russell, Minnesota Power chairman and chief executive officer, resigned.

Trouble for the region's taconite industry began on May 24, 2000, when LTV Steel Mining Company announced that it was closing its Hoyt Lakes taconite facility. Before the year ended, Wheeling-Pittsburgh Steel Company, one of the industry's major integrated producers, had filed for Chapter 11 bankruptcy protection. Even more threatening to the region's taconite economy was the continuing importation of foreign iron and steel. In 2000, some 15 million tons of pig iron and semi-finished steel slabs entered the United States, eliminating the need for about 20 million tons of taconite pellets.

Frank Ongaro had a front row seat for the taconite industry's first major setback of the 21st century. The Hibbing native was named executive director of the Iron Mining Association of Minnesota in early May 2000. "What had been kind of a stable, quiet resurgence in the 1990s in iron ore in northeastern Minnesota all of a sudden went into free fall," Ongaro said. "Two days before I officially started in this position, LTV announced that they would be closing their Hoyt Lakes, 1,400-plus employee taconite plant. And you can imagine the media scramble, political scramble and all of the other issues surrounding that from the region's standpoint.

"The old saying, 'We live in interesting times,' in the early part of this millennium was interesting with a capital "I" for iron ore in northeastern Minnesota," Ongaro said. "In a short couple of years, LTV closed its plant; National Steel filed bankruptcy; most, if not all, of Cleveland-Cliffs' owned or managed properties reduced staff or cut back production; EVTAC mining lost its largest customer, eventually went bankrupt, and closed its doors. And all of a sudden, there were a lot fewer plants operating and certainly a significant reduction in production of iron ore from northeastern Minnesota."

Through its key account management program, MP again worked with taconite customers to make energy usage as cost-efficient as possible.

Energy costs comprised about a quarter of the total cost of making pellets in 2000 and made up the second largest cost component for the industry after labor. Electric power costs comprised 60 percent of the typical taconite plant's energy costs.

Ongaro noted that taconite plant executives had come to appreciate MP's willingness to lobby the Minnesota Legislature to help its Large Power customers.

"When Minnesota Power goes to the state Legislature and makes sure that elected officials and administrative officials understand that increased costs would have a negative impact on the industry, it is extremely important to all the iron ore operators," Ongaro said. "And it's important for the simple reason that those costs cannot be borne by the industry alone. It's extremely important to the industry to make sure that unnecessary cost is not passed on to the operators."

The closure of LTV presented MP with a strategic opportunity to buy electric generation in its service area at a reasonable cost. About nine months after the LTV mining operation initiated a Chapter 11 bankruptcy proceeding and closed its plant in Hoyt Lakes, MP and Cleveland-Cliffs announced a purchase agreement. Cliffs acquired the taconite processing plant along with property related to mining operations.

A wholly owned subsidiary of MP, Rainy River Energy Corp.-Taconite Harbor, agreed to pay $75 million to LTV and Cliffs to acquire non-mining properties from LTV Steel Mining Co. These included its 225-megawatt electric generating facility, an existing coal pile, a 60-mile transmission line connecting the facility to the Iron Range, railroad trackage rights and about 30,000 acres of forest and recreation land in northeast Minnesota.

"Although the closure of LTV and the layoff of its work force was a serious blow to the regional economy, we were able to retain many jobs at the generating station," Eric Norberg said. As part of the transaction, MP donated properties near Hoyt Lakes and Giants Ridge for public recreation.

"We were able to upgrade the generating facility and put it back on-line just a year later," Norberg added. "The Taconite Harbor Generating Station continues to provide critical electric service to existing industrial plants in the region and we expect it to be a key part of our resource mix for years to come."

Power Line Politics

While MP's key account management personnel were working with taconite customers to help them recover from the latest downturn in the nation's iron and steel economy, other MP staffers were routing a power line across northwestern Wisconsin. The approximately 250-mile Wausau-Duluth line drew heated opposition from rural residents located along its right-of-way.

Jerry Ostroski was part of the team that had met with Governor Tommy Thompson, representatives of Wisconsin Public Service (WPS) and the other major Wisconsin utilities to plan a 345,000-volt transmission line from the Arrowhead Substation near Duluth to the WPS Weston Generating Station in central Wisconsin. For Ostroski, there was a personal component to the project.

"There's a steam plant in Weston that will be about the equivalent of Clay Boswell," Ostroski said. "They're building Unit No. 4 there, a 500-megawatt unit. So there'll be a clone of the Clay Boswell station down there when they finish the plant. And it's located on and next to the farm that my mother grew up on."

No one in Wisconsin or Minnesota state government seriously questioned the need for the new power line, and it seemed to be headed for quick regulatory approval. But in late 2000, grassroots opposition from environmentalists, farmers and county boards of commission in rural northwest Wisconsin pushed the power line into the headlines.

Workers erect a tower in northern Wisconsin for the Arrowhead-Weston high-voltage transmission line, bringing northwest Wisconsin one step closer to alleviating its persistent electric power shortage.

Led by Save Our Unique Lands (SOUL), a Mosinee, Wisconsin-based advocacy group, protesters attended county board meetings along the line's route to express their displeasure. Working with its partners, American Transmission Company (ATC) and WPS, MP answered critics' charges and concerns. By the summer of 2001, the Public Service Commission of Wisconsin had unanimously approved the construction of the line. During 2002 and 2003, ATC and WPS met with county boards and landowners to brief them on the line. The next two years were dedicated to detailed route and site preparation.

In 2005, the 12-mile Minnesota portion of the Arrowhead-Weston line was completed and construction on the Wisconsin portion got underway. The estimated finish date for the entire project is the spring of 2008.

Deb Amberg worked on the line from the beginning. An ALLETE environmental attorney, she brought a different perspective to the project. "My favorite story about the Arrowhead-Weston power line was that my son was born in September 1998," Amberg said. "I returned to work in December 1998 and heard that we were working on a new power line project. I'd done one power line earlier, a much smaller one, and it's a challenging process. But it's a great opportunity to bring a lot of diverse interests together, to work with a lot of different parts of the Company."

"My son started kindergarten last year," she said. "He's in first grade now, and the project's still not done. Sometimes things take longer than we think they're going to take, and certainly, building a 220-mile power line, a high-voltage power line of unprecedented size and scope for this area, is a big project. And we haven't built any major power lines for 20 years."

Because of changing societal demands, the power line also cost far more than the partners first estimated. "Things are a lot more expensive because we pay more attention to a lot more things than we used to," Amberg explained.

"This all takes time. It all takes money, and it takes paying attention to a lot of small details. Things take longer and they cost a lot more than they used to. Not that things are bad, but they've changed."

Amberg was named vice president, general counsel and secretary in 2004.

ALLETE's participation in the Arrowhead-Weston line brought it into a close relationship with American Transmission Company (ATC), its partner on the Wisconsin high-voltage line. A Wisconsin-based public utility that owns and maintains electric transmission assets in parts of the Badger State as well as neighboring Illinois and Michigan, ATC was actively seeking investment partners to help it expand operations in the Upper Midwest.

In December 2005, ALLETE announced that it intended to invest $60 million in ATC, an estimated nine-percent ownership interest in the powerline firm. In May 2006, the Public Service Commission of Wisconsin approved the investment, which ALLETE planned to make through its Wisconsin subsidiary, Rainy River Energy Corporation-Wisconsin.

ALLETE CEO Don Shippar noted that the investment in ATC was "consistent with our strategy of investing in utility-related opportunities in our region."

New Leadership

While Minnesota Power and its partners were attempting to put out fires related to the power line in northwestern Wisconsin in 2001, things began to heat up for the Board of Directors. On August 28, 2001—just two weeks before al-Qaida operatives piloted jetliners into the World Trade Center and the Pentagon—ALLETE's Board of Directors replaced Ed Russell with David Gartzke. A protégé of Arend Sandbulte and a 25-year veteran of the utility's finance operations, Gartzke was named ALLETE's president. Arend Sandbulte, who remained a member of the ALLETE Board, was asked to assume the additional duties of interim chairman.

Russell resigned after six years as ALLETE's president, CEO and chairman. He had been thinking about transition over the summer that year. The Company was in excellent shape with a talented management team in place, so it was a good time to make a change.

Russell's last year at the helm involved a bit of controversy. A staff member at Great Lakes Aquarium in Duluth, where Russell was a board member, wrote a letter to the editor at the *Duluth News Tribune* that was sharply critical of the Arrowhead-Weston transmission line. Russell then wrote a letter to the Aquarium's executive director objecting to the statements about the power line. Shortly after, the staff member left the Aquarium to pursue other interests.

Also that year, Russell resigned from Duluth's United Way board. Being a former Boy Scout, he was angered by United Way's decision to pull funding from the Scouts because the organization refused to sanction gay scouts or leaders.

John Cirello, the manager of the utility's Florida water operations, also left the Company at this time. Donnie Crandell, the architect of much of the ALLETE diversification effort, was asked to replace Cirello as head of the Company's Florida water facilities.

ADESA and Automotive Services

America and the world reeled from the horror of 9/11. By early fall, U.S. troops were on the ground in Afghanistan, uprooting the Taliban government that had given succor and support to al-Qaida.

But in the two weeks between the Russell resignation and the destruction of the World Trade Center, Gartzke and the ALLETE Board had to face a nagging issue. Almost the first question that the business media asked Gartzke concerned the diversified utility's lagging stock price.

Would ALLETE's new president advocate spinning off ADESA to restore Wall Street confidence?

It was a good question, but one rife with irony. At the time of Russell's resignation, ALLETE common stock was languishing in the $25 to $26 per share range. Utility analysts estimated the breakup value of the stock at $35 or more. Some analysts said they thought ADESA itself would trade at $20 or more a share.

The irony implicit in the question was the fact that ADESA was a major reason that ALLETE common stock traded so low. Most of the Wall Street analysts simply didn't understand how to value an electric utility that owned an auto auction company.

ADESA's continuing rapid growth in the 21st century convinced ALLETE to spin off the automobile auction firm in a 2004 initial public offering.

Even more galling to Wall Street was the fact that many utilities that had gone overseas to acquire foreign generation and transmission assets often had lost significant amounts of money. "A lot of those companies that went to Australia and to the Ukraine and to England to buy generation assets," Sandbulte said, "have had their head handed to them, many of them, and lost billions of dollars."

By the time of Russell's resignation, ADESA was one of ALLETE's most profitable ventures. In 2001, ADESA was the second largest wholesale vehicle auction firm in North America with 53 wholesale auction sites in the United States and Canada. The firm handled in excess of 1.3 million vehicles a year. The company reported operating revenues of $832 million, $310 million more than in 2000 and $212 million more than ALLETE's energy services division reported in operating revenues. Net income from automotive services was nearly $75 million in 2001, a 50-percent increase from 2000 and more than 54 percent of ALLETE's total net income for the year. Automotive Finance Corp. (AFC), the financing arm of ADESA, financed more than 900,000 vehicles in 2001, a 14-percent gain over the previous year.

What was perhaps most impressive about ADESA was its performance in the wake of 9/11. When most companies were struggling in the midst of some of the worst uncertainty to grip the nation since the early days of World War II, ADESA was thriving. Same-store sales at ADESA wholesale auctions increased 13 percent over 2000 levels. Automotive services comprised 46 percent of ALLETE assets by 2000.

But Wall Street had decided that a utility and an automobile auction were an incompatible combination. The decision set in motion another transformation of ALLETE. In 2004, directors approved a plan to spin off ADESA as a stand-alone company. As part of the initial public offering, they awarded ALLETE shareholders with a one-for-one distribution of ADESA stock. They also established a one-for-three reverse split for ALLETE stock that quickly resulted in the parent company's stock trading again in the $50 range.

Capital Re and Florida Land

The early years of the new millennium were a boom time for ALLETE's investments, including its partly owned reinsurance venture and its Florida land developments.

ALLETE's investment in Capital Re Corporation, the reinsurance company that Minnesota Power had helped form in 1988, ended with the 20th century. On December 30, 1999, shareholders of Capital Re voted to merge with ACE Limited, a much larger reinsurance company.

ALLETE's 7.3 million shares of Capital Re common shares was a 20 percent ownership in the reinsurance company. ALLETE exchanged

A 180-slip marina at Cape Coral in southwest Florida was one of the properties that ALLETE developed and later sold.

its shares for 4.7 million shares of ACE Limited common stock, plus a cash payment of just over $25 million. Based on the December 29, 1999 closing price of ACE Limited common shares of $16.75, the total value of ALLETE's proceeds in the transaction was $104.4 million.

In May 2000, ALLETE recorded a $30.4 million after tax gain on the sale of its 4.7 million shares of ACE Limited. Coupled with the $25.1 million cash payment the utility had received at the time of the sale in 1999, ALLETE's profit from its investment in Capital Re totaled more than $55 million. As a result of the merger, ALLETE in 1999 reported 52 cents a share, after tax, non-cash earnings on the transaction.

Laura Holquist, president of ALLETE Properties and Bill Livingston, president of Palm Coast Holdings survey the construction of a Publix grocery store at Town Center in ALLETE's Palm Coast development in northeast Florida, June 2006.

In the early 2000s, growth in ALLETE's investment sector was being fueled by the Company's Florida land development portfolio. Between 1996 and 1999, the Company made two major acquisitions in Florida, Palm Coast and Cape Coral.

Laura Holquist moved to Fort Myers in 1993 as the Company's vice president of finance for real estate sales at Lehigh Corporation. A Wisconsin native, Holquist had joined Minnesota Power's audit department in 1987. In 1990, she moved to the Company's corporate development department, where she worked on the team that did due diligence on the Lehigh Corporation acquisition. With increasing concern from Duluth about financial controls at Lehigh, Holquist was asked to transfer to Florida.

"At the time, we were looking at real estate as a temporary investment," she said. "The plan was to liquidate the real estate in five years' time. I was on a two- to four-year rotation. The thought was I'd go to Indianapolis for two years following my assignment in Fort Myers."

Ed Russell's arrival in 1995 put ALLETE solidly into the real estate business. Russell encouraged the corporate development staff to aggressively seek further Florida acquisitions. In 1996, ITT Corporation was in the process of breaking up. The company owned extensive timber lands it was converting into a planned unit development in Flagler County about halfway between St. Augustine and Daytona. ALLETE bought the development, Palm Coast, along with about 15,000 acres of land.

In 1999, ALLETE added another asset to its Florida real estate holdings when it purchased residential, commercial and recreational properties at Cape Coral on the Sunshine State's Gulf Coast. The $36 million purchase from Avatar Holdings included some 2,500 acres of commercially and residentially zoned land, along with marinas and a golf course.

The waterfront and golf course were "the real diamonds in the rough," Holquist said. "Cape Coral had key waterfront development property and 8,000 lots."

Holquist, who had been named senior vice president of ALLETE's Florida real estate development subsidiary, moved into sales in 2000. She sold a 180-slip marina development and soon was put in charge of sales for all of ALLETE's southwest Florida properties. In 2001, Holquist helped ALLETE acquire its first shopping center in Winterhaven and began developing a regional retail site, Town Center at Palm Coast. Holquist and the staff also began planning Ormond Crossing, a new mixed-use development north of Daytona.

In 2001, Holquist was named president of ALLETE's real estate services division.

Transformation

2004 was a year of metamorphosis for ALLETE. In mid-year, the utility sold its North Carolina water and wastewater treatment assets, as well as the remaining 72 water and wastewater systems in Florida. The proceeds from the sale of all of the utility's water and wastewater facilities came to approximately $300 million, after deducting transaction costs, retirement of debt and payment of taxes.

"Regulation had been getting tighter and tighter," explained Donnie Crandell, who had been named president of Florida Water in 2001. "And there were an increasing number of Florida local governments interested in buying our systems. The Board tried to sell the whole thing, but the courts threw that out. We ended up selling Florida Water off in pieces. But we got a very good price for it."

A technician monitors the flow at a community served by Florida Water.

ALLETE also received an excellent price for its investment in ADESA. On September 20, 2004, ALLETE spun off the automotive services business by distributing to ALLETE shareholders all of the utility's shares of ADESA common stock.

Earlier that summer, ALLETE had completed an ADESA IPO through the issuance and sale of 6.3 million shares of the auto auction company's stock. As part of the IPO and spin-off, ALLETE received a $100 million dividend and the repayment of all intercompany debt from ADESA.

Using internally generated funds and proceeds from the sale of the water and wastewater system and the ADESA IPO, ALLETE paid down more than $500 million in debt in 2003 and 2004.

The 2004 transformation prepared ALLETE for new directions under new leadership at the dawn of its second century of operations.

CHAPTER 15 At the Dawn of a Second Century

ALLETE ended the final year of its first century of operation with new leadership. David Gartzke, who had guided the Company from late 2001 through the ADESA IPO, elected to move to Indianapolis in 2004 as president, CEO and chairman of the automobile auction company.

Gartzke's successor as ALLETE president and CEO was a utility veteran with experience in a host of job assignments, including telecommunications technology, diversification, human resources, utility operations and labor relations. Donald Shippar never intended to pursue a utility career when he was growing up in Superior, across St. Louis Bay from Duluth.

"I went to Superior Senior High School," Shippar explained, "and when I got out of high school, I went to Wisconsin Indianhead Technical Institute and got an A.A. degree in electronics technology. I actually started to work in the broadcast industry. And that's how I ended up in Upper Michigan. I worked for WLUC-TV in Marquette as a broadcast engineer. My wife and I were up there probably nine months and then we had an opportunity to move back to Duluth. I went to work for what was then KDAL-TV—now KDLH-TV—and worked there for about six years as a broadcast engineer."

ALLETE Chairman, President and CEO Don Shippar (right) was joined by Minnesota Governor Tim Pawlenty at the kick-off of Minnesota Power's Centennial celebration on February 9, 2006.

Shippar might have stayed at the Duluth CBS-TV affiliate for his entire career had Minnesota Power not experienced the growth it did in the mid-1970s. Admittedly restless because advancement opportunities were limited at the television station, he began investigating work possibilities at the local utility.

Minnesota Power was "building a lot of new generation stations and also doing a lot of automation," Shippar said, "particularly in the telecommunications area. They were building their own microwave system, putting in a whole new control system across the network, and as a result of that, the Company was hiring a lot of people at the time in many different areas, especially engineering technicians and operating people."

Shippar was hired in 1976 as a technician in Minnesota Power's meter and test department. Shortly after he started, Shippar transferred to the Company's Energy Control Center in Duluth, now Rowe Energy Control Center. Minnesota Power at the time was installing a new computer system to control all of the substations, as well as the transmission and distribution lines across the system.

"I got involved in that effort and started to work up there," Shippar said. "A short time later I applied for and was successful in getting a supervisory position that in essence was responsible for coordinating much of the field installation of the new equipment. So I spent several years working in the field, going around to all the different stations, generating stations and substations, installing equipment and bringing it online as we installed the new control system in parallel with the old system."

In the early 1980s, Bob Marchetti, then Minnesota Power's senior vice president, asked Shippar to take the reins at JayEn, the Hermantown telecommunications firm that had been one of the utility's first diversification ventures. Shippar was instrumental in helping Minnesota Power find new ownership for JayEn, and 18 months later, he returned to the parent company.

Shippar moved to 30 West Superior Street where he worked the next four years as director of labor relations in the human resources department. During the early 1980s, he negotiated the labor agreements with Local 31 of the International Brotherhood of Electrical Workers (IBEW). In 1985, Chuck Wood, the human resources director at the time, transferred to Southern States Utilities. Shippar subsequently was promoted to director of human resources, a job he held for seven years. In the mid-1980s, he graduated summa cum laude from the University of Wisconsin-Superior with a B.S. degree in business and economics.

In the early 1990s, Minnesota Power reorganized its work practices and assignments. Shippar transferred to distribution services. "I was responsible for all the line crews and the maintenance group for the distribution system," Shippar said. "It was what is now called our retail customer service, which would be all our residential-commercial reps and the call center/ billing area. I was working up at the Herbert Service Center."

Pat Mullen, a Proctor native who worked his way up from a sales clerk at The Electric Outlet to head ALLETE's customer service efforts, worked with Shippar to transform Minnesota Power's distribution functions. "It was in early 1996 when Don Shippar, who was vice president of distribution and transmission, and Steve Sherner, who was the vice president of marketing, got a team together to evaluate how that part of the business should be organized," Mullen said.

"There was a transition of my customer service group from marketing to distribution operations. Don Shippar was my vice president, and we were looking at the efficiency and productivity of the customer service function as it relates to line workers and field operations. So it was 1996 when we started what we called internally a distribution company, which had all the field operations and all customer service activities. It's an important piece of how we put all your services under one roof."

Minnesota Power then added the transmission system operations group to Shippar's responsibility area. He soon was named a vice president, overseeing the Company's distribution and transmission operations. In 2000, Shippar was named executive vice president and chief operating officer of Minnesota Power.

"We were responsible for transmission, distribution, customer service and the generation side of the business," Shippar said. "In essence, I took care of the operating segments of the utility, everything with the exception of accounting, finance and support services."

In 2003, Shippar was named president of Minnesota Power. "When we prepared to spin off ADESA, I was named president and CEO of ALLETE. At the time the IPO was completed in September 2004, the board wanted to make it clear that we had planned to separate the companies so Dave Gartzke could focus full time on the spin-off of ADESA. The board wanted him to get prepared to move to Indianapolis and start running the Company full time."

ALLETE Board Chairman Bruce Stender shares a light moment with fellow board member George Mayer.

Shippar worked closely through the transition with ALLETE's new chairman of the board. Bruce Stender had joined the Company's board in 1995. The former president of the College of St. Scholastica and president of a Duluth-based hospitality company, Labovitz Enterprises, Stender was intrigued by the opportunity to sit on the utility's board.

"I got a phone call in early 1995 or late 1994 from Arend Sandbulte,"

Stender said, "and Sandy asked if he could come and visit with me. He did, and he said he would like me to consider a seat on the Minnesota Power Board. Obviously, this was a very flattering invitation, one that I thought very seriously about, and did make the commitment to stand for election at the 1995 shareholder meeting. And it has been a real highlight of my life to be able to participate in the growth and development of Minnesota Power in this short 10-year period of its 100-year existence. It's been a wonderful opportunity to see corporate life in our region grow and develop and change, as all successful corporations must do."

Global Realities

The ALLETE that greeted Stender and Shippar in 2004 had changed dramatically since 2000. Once again primarily an electric utility, ALLETE's major diversification asset was the portfolio of Florida land properties.

The firm's electric utility served a region that also had changed dramatically since 2000. After surviving the upheaval caused by the 2000 closure of the LTV Mine, and later the bankruptcy and closure of Eveleth Taconite (EVTAC), the Mesabi roared back in 2004 and 2005, the beneficiary of surging global demand for iron ore and metallics. Much of the demand was fueled by China's steel industry, which quietly became the world's largest early in the century. In 2003 and 2004, Chinese steelmakers came all the way to Minnesota to meet that demand.

Frank Ongaro, the executive director of the Iron Mining Association of Minnesota, pointed out that Chinese interest in Mesabi Range taconite dated back to about 2000. "Back when EVTAC mining was losing its largest customer, the then president of the company, Howard Hilshorst, said he was approached through Congressman Oberstar's office from some interests representing the Chinese steel company."

The Chinese interest was Laiwu Steel, a major producer in the Asian market, and Laiwu was interested in securing North American supplies of iron ore. The Chinese producer approached Cleveland-Cliffs Inc about a partnership in 2004. Laiwu and Cleveland-Cliffs announced the formation of a joint venture partnership, United Taconite, to purchase, reopen and operate the EVTAC property.

Ongaro recalled first hearing the rumor that the Chinese were interested in acquiring a Minnesota taconite mining facility. "Everybody sitting around the room, I recall, scoffed at that a bit, saying 'OK, yeah, that'll be the day that that happens.' If two and a half years ago, somebody would have said a steel company from China was going to come to northeastern Minnesota and buy a taconite plant, you would have locked that person in a rubber room."

Ongaro credited James L. Oberstar, Minnesota's 8th District congressman, with having the vision to put Laiwu and Cleveland-Cliffs together as partners in the United Taconite joint venture.

"Significant credit certainly goes to Mr. Oberstar for pushing the envelope, hosting meetings with the Chinese consulate and bringing in these individuals who might have interest, and then eventually building those relationships with the Laiwu executives," Ongaro said. "Obviously, Cleveland-Cliffs took a bold move to look at the acquisition of assets for what turned out to be a very positive future marketplace for them."

The increasing global character of the iron and steel business was manifested in several other events in 2003 and 2004. While United Taconite was returning the EVTAC property to commercial production, USX's Minntac mine quietly was shipping taconite pellets by rail to Vancouver for shipment to China. Hibbing Taconite Company and Inland Steel Mining Company, two of the stronger producers on the Iron Range, were acquired by Indian steelmaker Lakshmi Mittal when he made ISG Corp. and Inland Steel part of his Mittal Steel Group.

Dave McMillan, executive vice president, recounted Minnesota Power's proud history as part of his Master of Ceremonies duty at the Company's Centennial kick-off celebration.

Dave McMillan, MP executive vice president, said globalization and concentration of ownership have transformed Minnesota Power's large industrial customer base.

"We had seven taconite mines up here when I started dealing with Large Power customers," he said. "There were probably eight, nine or possibly 10 different corporate entities, if you think of Oglebay Norton and Hanna Mining Company and those types of players. They're all gone now, down to USX operating two of the plants, and Cliffs effectively operating three of the plants including Northshore Mining, United Taconite and Hibbing Taconite. And then you've got Mittal. While there are still a few non-operating owners, three corporate entities are running six mines. Paper is even more globalized, in that paper is a commodity that can move around the world a little bit easier than steel."

The global Large Power customer base has never lost its importance for ALLETE's bottom line, even during the height of the Company's diversification initiative in the 1990s. "We're very competitive in providing power to a home," McMillan explained. "Yet in reality, the homes in the region only comprise one-sixth of our load. One-sixth is residential, one-sixth is commercial and two-thirds is large industrial and municipal. So big accounts that take big amounts of electricity remain the backbone of ALLETE's operations—as they have for the better part of our first century."

A Bright Future

Short-term expansion of northern Minnesota's global iron and paper resources is likely in the years ahead, McMillan noted. "Maybe there's more investment opportunity, who knows. But 10 years ago there was nothing. Expansion wasn't even a figment of anybody's imagination."

One likelihood is the development of an alternative iron technology on the Mesabi Range. "If iron ore could have its traditional blast furnace

The Taconite Harbor Energy Center at Schroeder, Minnesota will help meet retail demand in the Company's second century of operation.

market and at the same time start to develop a sizable piece of the business that's selling 97 percent or 98 percent iron products to the electric arc furnace business, then you've successfully diversified what the Iron Range depends upon."

McMillan said the Mesabi Nugget project remains promising, as does the potential of copper nickel development. "Any kind of manufacturing activity that's resource-based is going to have major secondary and tertiary ramifications for everybody in northeastern Minnesota other than just the vendors that sell to us," McMillan said. "Those are big deals for the regional economy, very important for Minnesota Power as you look at continued dependence on a small set of industrial customers."

One change already underway in 2006 was the redirection of output from the Taconite Harbor Energy Center from wholesale to retail sales.

The 225-megawatt Taconite Harbor generating asset had long served North Shore wholesale taconite customers with electric power. But with load growth of approximately 200 megawatts projected for 2010 and an additional 200 megawatts of growth anticipated for 2015, Minnesota Power determined in the fall of 2005 that demand growth in the region could best be met with the Taconite Harbor facilities.

In early 2006, the Minnesota Public Utilities Commission approved Minnesota Power's plans to shift the plant from wholesale to retail sales. At the same time, the Company said it would supplement output from Taconite Harbor with a 50-megawatt long-term purchase from Manitoba Hydro.

McMillan pointed out that the pulp and paper sector of the regional economy also has the potential to create more business for ALLETE and its electric utility. "We have a key account engineer working in Grand Rapids right now who's been doing nothing for the past year other than helping Blandin and UPM determine whether they can put a paper machine on the ground over there that would expand our load dramatically. We have similar arrangements with the paper customers to assure that we are doing everything possible to optimize their competitive position."

21st Century Opportunities

With its core energy business in stronger shape than at any time in the past quarter-century, ALLETE is poised for the kind of growth it enjoyed during the 1960s and 1970s. But according to Donald Shippar, that doesn't preclude the Company from embarking upon another round of diversification activity. Shippar pointed with pride to the success of the Company's Florida real estate portfolio and said that ALLETE would be alert to other such opportunities in the future.

"As we have for the past 25 years," he said, "we continue to look at ways to diversify ALLETE. We've been very straightforward with our investor community, our employees and our shareholders in telling them that, yes, we're going to concentrate on the energy business and electric business as well as Florida real estate. We're going to look for opportunities to grow those two businesses, but we're also going to look for other businesses. We're not just going to concentrate on those two segments of ALLETE. We continue to have a group of people internally that is actively looking for other businesses that would serve to diversify the Company and that would serve to grow the earnings of ALLETE going forward."

ALLETE will remain alert to diversification and investment

opportunities. Late in 2005, the Company announced its intentions to sell its subsidiary, Enventis Telecom, to Hickory Tech Corporation of Mankato for $35.5 million. ALLETE had hoped to grow Enventis into a $200 million firm. The way to do that was by acquiring other VoIP companies, but by 2004, prices had escalated dramatically.

"We made the decision to exit the business and sell it," Shippar said of the sale to Hickory Tech. "Bob Adams and his team had done a good, fairly fast track build from scratch. They took Enventis in five years from zero to $50 million. I think that Enventis shows that we've been very disciplined about getting into things and knowing when to get out."

Shippar said he remains "very optimistic about our future. There are a lot of opportunities out there. The market right now for acquiring new businesses is a tough one. There's a lot of money involved, there are a lot of competitors, and in our opinion, there are people perhaps paying too much for companies. But nevertheless, we're out there. We're looking, we're active, and I think it's just a matter of time before we find something that we think makes a good fit. When we do, we can proceed to take the next step in diversification—and to continue that long tradition that's been a part of ALLETE for so many years."

Celebrating 100 Years

To observe its 100th anniversary as an electric utility, Minnesota Power formed a charitable foundation early in 2006. Called the Minnesota Power Foundation, the new financial organization was set up to bring all the Company's philanthropic efforts under one name, establishing a more efficient and vibrant community organization.

Shippar noted that Minnesota Power in recent years has contributed nearly $1 million annually to worthwhile causes in northern Minnesota. He added that it is expected that the Foundation will continue that level of giving in coming years.

"It is important to direct our resources toward areas that matter most to those we serve," Shippar said. "The Foundation will focus its giving on grants that strengthen the community and enhance the quality of life for people served by Minnesota Power."

Shippar said he's positive that ALLETE can prosper and thrive into its second century of operations. He paid tribute to the creativity, dedication, ingenuity and work ethic of the people who work for ALLETE today, and the generations of Minnesota Power employees who built a tradition of excellence during the past 100 years. Those employees, past and present, combined an aptitude for technological innovation, financial conservatism, a willingness to take risks, an understanding of customer needs and a commitment to northeastern Minnesota's unique environment.

Those were the people responsible for Electrifying a Century.

Don Shippar rings the bell at the New York Stock Exchange in honor of Minnesota Power's Centennial. (Left to right: Vince Meyer, ALLETE senior financial analyst; Don Stellmaker, ALLETE treasurer; Catherine Kinney, NYSE president; Don Shippar, ALLETE chairman, president and CEO; Jim Vizanko, retired (6/06) ALLETE chief financial officer; and Tim Thorp, ALLETE vice president investor relations.)

Index